Local Management of Schools

Other Books in the Series

Emerging Partnerships: Current Research in Language and Literacy
DAVID WRAY (ed.)
The Management of Change
PAMELA LOMAX (ed.)
Managing Better Schools and Colleges
PAMELA LOMAX (ed.)
Managing Staff Development in Schools
PAMELA LOMAX (ed.)
Performance Indicators
C. T. FITZ-GIBBON (ed.)

Other Books of Interest

Breaking the Boundaries
EUAN REID and HANS H. REICH (eds)
Child Language Disability: Volumes I and II
KAY MOGFORD-BEVAN and JANE SADLER (eds)
Citizens of This Country: The Asian British
MARY STOPES-ROE and RAYMOND COCHRANE
Community Languages: A Handbook
BARBARA M. HORVATH and PAUL VAUGHAN
Continuing to Think: The British Asian Girl
BARRIE WADE and PAMELA SOUTER
Critical Theory and Classroom Talk
ROBERT YOUNG
Education for Work
DAVID CORSON (ed.)
Education of Chinese Children in Britain:
A Comparative Study with the United States of America
LORNITA YUEN-FAN WONG
Language Policy Across the Curriculum
DAVID CORSON
Life in Language Immersion Classrooms
ELIZABETH B. BERNHARDT (ed.)
One Europe - 100 Nations
ROY N. PEDERSEN
Parents on Dyslexia
S. van der STOEL (ed.)
Story as Vehicle
EDIE GARVIE
Teacher Supply and Teacher Quality
GERALD GRACE and MARTIN LAWN (eds)

Please contact us for the latest book information:
Multilingual Matters Ltd
Bank House, 8a Hill Road
Clevedon, Avon BS21 7HH
England

BERA Dialogues 6
Series Editor: Pamela Lomax

Local Management of Schools: Research and Experience

Edited by

Gwen Wallace

MULTILINGUAL MATTERS LTD
Clevedon • Philadelphia • Adelaide

Library of Congress Cataloging in Publication Data

Local Management of Schools: Research and Experience/Edited by Gwen Wallace
(BERA Dialogs: 6)
Includes bibliographical references.
1. School management and organization — Great Britain. I. Wallace, Gwen. II. Series.
LB2900.5.L63 1992
371.2'00941   dc20

British Library Cataloguing in Publication Data

A CIP catalogue record for this book is available from the British Library.

ISBN 1-85359-153-X (hbk)
ISBN 1-85359-152-1 (pbk)

Multilingual Matters Ltd

UK: Bank House, 8a Hill Road, Clevedon, Avon BS21 7HH, England.
USA: 1900 Frost Road, Suite 101, Bristol, PA 19007, USA.
Australia: PO Box 6025, 83 Gilles Street, Adelaide, SA 5000, Australia.

Typeset, printed and bound in Great Britain by the Longdunn Press Ltd.

Contents

Preface

Local Management of Schools: Research and Experience is the sixth in the present series of BERA Dialogues. BERA Dialogues is a publication of the British Educational Research Association (BERA). Royalties from the series go to BERA rather than to its authors and editors. BERA Dialogues was intended to extend the publications of BERA to provide an outlet for material that was different from that published in its journal, *British Educational Research Journal*, and its newsletter, *Research Intelligence*. Of the three criteria of difference, i.e.

> that special consideration will be given to material that falls outside the normal conventions applied by academic journals with regard to content, style, length and format;

> that special consideration will be given to collections of material from people who do not normally publish in academic journals; and

> that special consideration will be given to the need for urgency in publication on key educational issues,

it is the last one that applies to Dialogues 6.

Gwen Wallace has edited a collection of accounts that addresses one of the most far-reaching changes in British education this century, and one (she argues) that has attracted little press comment. Although there are a number of books about local management of schools (LMS), they have tended to approach the subject from a management perspective rather than from a research perspective. Gwen's book draws upon the organisation and resource of BERA. Her material is illuminated by her work as convenor of a BERA Policy Task Group working in the area of LMS and providing a focus for a network of concerned practitioners. The accounts presented in the book were developed at the 1990 Annual BERA Conference and in a BERA Regional Research Seminar that took place in Derbyshire in November 1990.

Pamela Lomax
Series Editor

1 Introduction: The Organisation and the Teacher

GWEN WALLACE

Introduction

Schools are now 'in the market'. Formula funding, largely based on pupil numbers, is designed to make the popular school rich and the unpopular non-viable. Legislation for 'open access' in the 1988 Education Reform Act (ERA), means that efficient schools, with high standards, are expected to thrive and expand, as the inefficient close down for lack of pupils. Associated changes in educational policy require teachers to 'deliver' the national curriculum, assess their pupils' progress at 7, 11, 14 and 16, and, depending on local authority policies for phasing in the changes, take over the management of their own budgets. It is this last aspect of government policy — budget delegation based on formula funding — which, although it inevitably embraces all the rest, is commonly known as local management of schools (LMS).

The national curriculum has had the advantage of widespread comment, some of which has brought modifications to the proposed syllabuses. The nation-wide introduction of the standard assessment tasks (SATs) for seven-year-olds is under way as I write (April 1991), and has hit the headlines several times. Controversy surrounding their pilot stage, resulted in the reduction of the number and scope of the tasks. This has been followed, most recently, by a majority vote (not yet activated) of teachers at the 1991 Annual Conference of the National Union of Teachers, on a resolution not to implement them. There is some parental opposition to testing but this is much more vocal and widespread in the Scottish system.

LMS, however, proceeds apace attracting little public notice. Schools which opt out of local authority control into grant maintained (GM) status, funded directly from central government, are rather more likely to make headline news in the local and, on occasion, national press than those which stay with local authority control under LMS. Yet, there has been little debate on the budget issues. Even the Secretary of State's decision to extend the Act's provisions to allow the smallest primary and special schools to opt for local management, provoked little interest.

Without speculating on the reasons for this, this volume is a small attempt to remedy the situation. As a major educational innovation, LMS is placing unprecedented pressure on the way schools and local authorities work. It is also inevitably changing the questions for educational research. The in-service training (INSET) accompanying LMS is encouraging heads and deputies to set objectives, plan, implement, evaluate and revise their practices, both as budget managers *and* as reflective practitioners. There is also an increasing demand for INSET in research methods, and a developing constituency of 'action-researchers' among classroom teachers using a similar model for reviewing their classroom practices.

On the one hand, then, the ERA offers an imposed curricula and assessment structure; on the other it decentralises and delegates local powers of management to each individual school.

This is not the place for a full review of the ERA. More comprehensive coverage of its provisions and social and political context, can be found in Flude & Hammer (1990). Here we need only note that LMS is not an isolated policy change but part of a comprehensive range of legislation designed to change the way schools work. The complex mix of interests — financial, administrative and educational — shaped by the opportunities and limitations enshrined in the legislation, come together in the school development plan (SDP). The identification of new objectives, and, in turn, their implementation, evaluation and revision, will now take place in an environment where budgeting has assumed a new status. Schools are under a statutory obligation to implement the national curriculum and carry out national programmes of assessment. Planning is predominently about managing the statutory requirements, within the financial limitations. Given the legislation for open access, schools must aim to be both financially viable and educationally effective, demonstrating this effectiveness and efficiency to parents — not least through the publication of their assessment results — in order to attract and retain pupils. Hence, the argument goes, the loop closes because schools and parents will have shared purposes and common goals. It is not surprising, then, that a major question to emerge in the following chapters addresses the claim that, under market conditions, such a common interest between providers and consumers of schooling will emerge.

My aim in bringing these papers together, as convenor of the LMS Task

Group of the British Educational Research Association, has been to produce a volume which is accessible to the non-specialist, as well as the specialist, without compromising the integrity demanded of researchers for critical and systematic enquiry. I hope it offers a medium for communicating complex issues to interested teachers, governors, local authority administrators, parents and others, which will be both informative and readable. A wide-ranging public debate is already overdue.

One positive side of budget delegation, and the accompaning need for schools and teachers to account for what they are doing, is that it acts as a spur to policy-related and action research, thereby broadening the base of professional knowledge. Furthermore, it is also opening up new questions about schooling to researchers from other traditions.

This volume provides a case in point. As well as including contributions from eminent, long-time researchers into education, it has papers written by: Local Education Authority (LEA) administrators; a primary school teacher who only recently moved into higher education; and several recruits to educational research from backgrounds in social policy, management, industrial relations, accountancy and finance.

In this chapter, I first provide a basic guide to the rules for formula funding which, under the terms of the ERA, have established the centrally defined structure of financial limits within which schools must self-manage themselves locally. I then go on to summarise the subsequent chapters.

The Basics of Formula Funding

Every LEA has a general schools budget (GSB), some of which, like capital expenditure on buildings, cannot be devolved. The rest is called the aggregated schools budget (ASB).[1] Under LMS, at least 75% of this year's and 80% of next year's ASB must be delegated to schools. LEAs may, however, retain up to 10% of their ASB (falling to 7% after three years) for central services. Delegation is according to a formula based on age-weighted pupil units (AWPUs). Each LEA's scheme for delegation must be approved by the Department of Education and Science (DES). Implementation may be staged over a period of four years from April 1990.

Details of the current schemes have been analysed by Thomas (1990) who provides a good general guide to the whole subject. For our purposes we need note only that LEAs have had some discretion in deciding on the age bands and their relative weightings, on how much money over and above the 75% they have delegated, and on how far they have used their discretionary 25% to supplement a school's funds. Discretion may work by the use of additional weightings in favour of pupils with special needs or be used to redress other disadvantages experienced by small schools (see both Stewart and Lee in this volume).

Beyond this, Thomas (1990: 32) identifies 'a consensus' on the issues regarded as most important. These are:

- the mandatory discrepancy between teachers' actual salary costs and a formula based upon the average salary, a matter over which LEAs have no choice
- the debate over items retained as central services (especially funding for special needs)
- the percentage of GSB delegated to schools
- the need to be seen to be fair in the distribution of delegated funds
- the form of protection given to small schools (which have higher costs)
- the relative funding of primary as against secondary schools
- the decisions surrounding the need for training and support systems and plans for monitoring and evaluation.

The areas of discretion have led to some significant differences between LEAs but, as Thomas shows, the differences between authorities do not reflect party political principles. More interestingly, the greatest pressure appears to come from the 'need to maintain the status quo as far as possible' (Thomas, 1990: 6).

The two most disputed aspects of the formula are those which set limits on local authority options. First is the limit of 10% of GSB retainable by LEAs, which must reduce to 7% over three years and which LEAs claim is too small for central services. Central services may include museums, libraries, educational psychologists, some INSET, and structural maintenance and repairs. Second is the use of the average teacher's salary for calculating each school's staffing costs, rather than the actual cost of each school's staff salaries (see, for example, O'Connor, 1989; Wootton, 1989). This is contentious because it takes no account of historic differences between schools or their staffing profiles. Nevertheless, given the overall sum delegated according to formula, there is scope at school level to vire funds across budget heads to create different priorities.

LMS legislation also encourages internal markets between schools, and between schools and local authority, although Thomas (1990: 32) found the idea of 'buying in' services not widely accepted. The major problem this creates for the LEAs is that schools may choose not to buy, finding other priorities more pressing or other suppliers more attractive. Schools may also contract with other parties for all kinds of services. They may let out buildings and supply secretarial services. Most notably, through prospectuses, examination results and the general 'image' they present, heads have been nurtured in the belief that they will need to 'market' their schools to maintain or raise the numerical base of pupils on roll and guarantee their income. Finally, as a means of enhancing choice and freeing schools from the strait-jacket of local authority control, schools may supplement the funds allocated by the formula, with money raised by any variety of legal means.

The basic principles of formula funding and budget delegation, establish what government legislation has approved as the 'equitable' grounds on which local authorities and their schools should compete 'in the market'. I turn now to a brief overview of the contributions in the book in order to illustrate the dilemmas, challenges and problems in practice.

Experience and Research

The next three chapters draw on experience at the sharp end of practice. In Chapter 2, Mike Stewart draws on his experience in managing the delegation of budgets to schools in South Kent to fill out the LMS scenario with a real life example. Noting the crucial difference between the schemes which piloted budget delegation, based on historic budgets, and the final South Kent scheme based on a formula through which most schools lost funding, he describes the reasoning behind the weightings the LEA gave to different groups and puts real flesh on the basics outlined above. Evidence of the favourable response by heads to the powers they gained is somewhat countered by the formidable burden of administration shouldered by headteachers and their secretaries. Stewart's view is that LMS represents a challenge to schools to 'balance' the obligation to provide the curriculum to which pupils are entitled by virtue of the funding each brings, against the overall income from formula funding. Illustrating the scope and the complexity of the obligations placed on heads and governors, and recognising the current threat to the very existence of LEAs posed by government encouragement to schools to opt out of local authority control, he nevertheless views the scene positively, believing the balance is being achieved.

In Chapter 3, Margaret Maden writes from the experience of a chief education officer, and offers a critical and systematic agenda for researchers. She challenges many of the assumptions in the ERA legislation, calling on researchers to 'unpack' them. Her first challenge is for an examination of the consequences of the DES claim to fund pupil needs, when it has ruled that formula must be based on age weightings. Secondly, she questions the claim that delegation of powers will, of itself, improve the quality of teaching and learning. Her third area of concern is the quality and range of information schools require to make major policy decisions. The complexity of providing it and the skills required to use it well, particularly in the situation of tight budgetary constraint experienced by many schools which have lost out under the new system, raises huge questions about the likely consequences of LMS. Turning to the assumption that schools will be more responsive to clients, she raises the spectre of consumers with varying, even contrary expectations and hence queries the future for minority groups. Her final observations focus on the future of the local authority, reversing the assumption that a weaker LEA is a natural consequence of LMS.

Robert McGovern writes autobiographically, in Chapter 4, of the impact the preparations for LMS had on the school where he was deputy head. He recounts the hard lessons they had to learn as the promise of delegated powers faded before the reality that 75% of the school's budget was needed to cover staffing costs. The gains in power seemed insignificant when set against the increased workload, much of which devolved on to the underpaid secretary. Financial considerations eclipsed educational ones but with the undoubted benefit that governors became aware of the extent to which the school was underfunded. Willingly conceding the value of SDPs, he recalls the horror with which staff greeted the challenge they brought, and the relief which came with local authority support. In spite of school–LEA tensions, his school had no wish to opt out. Confounded by the reported enthusiasm for LMS in the pilot schools, he calls for formal evaluation and research.

In Chapter 5, we move into a research report. Analysing the way in which LMS represents but one facet of the ERA, Richard Bowe and Stephen Ball comment on the alien nature of the market mechanism to education. Locating the ideology in neo-liberal beliefs that the market copes best with rapid change (comparing favourably with state coercion), they test the consequences of the policy in a case study of one secondary school. Ironically, they observe the school's initial enthusiasm for local management coalesce into 'technocratic, hierarchical managerial styles' as decision making devolved to a small management team, largely isolated from the concerns of the rest of the school. Far from experiencing greater freedom of choice, the management team became more aware of their lack of negotiating power. They responded by tightening controls over school administration while taking on huge financial risks to get into the leisure market. Stewart's model of 'balance' in Chapter 2, emerges in Bowe & Ball's analysis as, 'expanded and contradictory sets of demands' which derive from government policy. Noting the time that trained teachers are having to spend on financial business, they call for a public debate on the role of teachers and the purposes of schooling.

From another part of the country, Jane Broadbent, Richard Laughlin, David Shearn and Nigel Dandy present not dissimilar evidence in Chapter 6. This time, the cases examined cover four, very different, schools. In setting the context, Broadbent *et al.* also highlight the way the ERA establishes accountability by linking formula funding to the national curriculum and assessment programmes and they argue that 'financial viability is being used as a proxy for educational viability'. Although practices differ from school to school, in general, the findings from their case studies also lead to the conclusion that LMS is being 'contained' by the head and very few others. They too note the 'high cost' as key senior staff are locked into routine, administrative tasks. Their theoretical arguments lead to the view that although the system has changed — in protecting most staff from the financial issues — heads have protected also the cultural 'lifeworlds' of the schools.

Tim Lee's focus, in Chapter 7, is on special needs. He notes the problems which stem from conflicting definitions and shows how 'special need' is commonly confused with 'social disadvantage'. By limiting the amount that LEAs can spend on children with special needs, the DES is undermining those children's traditional source of support. If LEAs are forced to become 'service agencies', then, Lee argues, the Coopers & Lybrand (1988) prediction of 'underpurchase' is more realistic than the Government's vision of a more effective and efficient service. For Lee, a major problem lies with the 'indefensible' way LEAs are being forced to find simple, objective definitions for a complex problem. Summing up, he too calls for a wide debate to address, 'the rival demands and the perverse incentives' which make LMS a 'major challenge' rather than a 'major opportunity'.

In Chapter 8, Rosalind Levačić, comes from a quite different perspective to model the balances, dilemmas and paradoxes she finds endemic in organisational co-ordination. Arguing that decentralisation, using the internal market mechanism, is a more effective means of organisational control than centralisation, she sets the boundaries for local managemtnt around the LEA and its schools. The LEA acts as a buyer of educational services through its power to determine, by formula, the price it places on different kinds of pupils' education, and the criteria by which it can discriminate between them. This is where the LEA holds its powers. However, it must also sell its services to schools, in competition with other agencies, in order to recover the money it has spent. Modelling the countervailing pressures of centralised, versus decentralised control she sees LMS fitting a pattern of organisation which separates strategic from operational decision making. The national curriculum and the assessment programmes fit into the picture as 'artificial targets' for regulating the market. Her study of Edmonton in Canada provides an interesting example of decentralised organisation.

However, she too notes the time required to cost, monitor and revise contracts, particularly for special needs. Another issue arises from the need to ensure that 'perverse incentives are not created which cause employees to act against the interests of the organisation'. Finally she points out that the decentralised arrangements legislated for LMS, unlike her Edmonton example, are not simply a matter of organisational decentralisation, but political decentralisation.

In Chapter 9, Ewart Keep continues with the market theme, echoing Lee's concern at the 'more simplistic attempts to equate schools with business'. Observing that marketplace theory is not the same as markets in practice, he questions the government's view that the market mechanism will ensure survival of the most efficient schools or promote perfect competition. In a survey of market realities, he raises several spectres, including those of cartels and cowboy firms. Schools can learn from industry, but only if industrial practices are critically analysed in all their complex variety. Arguing moreover, that 'random and conflicting elements' of different private sector management models are being embraced simultaneously, he finds confusion over what lessons education is supposed to learn from industry, who is supposed to be doing the learning and how responsibility is allocated. The styles and methods appropriate to managing the food industry are not necessarily appropriate for computers. Decentralised models may only be suitable for simple products and there is evidence of 'damaging long-term effects' of 'numbers-driven' rather than 'issue-driven' management. Noting that schools perform a service, rather than produce a product, he points out that the national curriculum was a strategic, political choice, not a matter of market research. The evidence that inappropriate styles of management end in failure leads him to advise circumspection.

Returning to the subject of schooling in Chapter 10, Marilyn Leask advocates the 'whole school approach to planning' through the use of SDPs. Following a brief review of current changes in curriculum and management, she recounts the story of the development of planning through the introduction of direct bidding and the direct funding of resources for Technical Vocational Education Initiative (TVEI) and INSET. Preparing the way for extending the idea into delegated budgets, the Coopers & Lybrand (1988) report, argued that LMS would succeed only if staff and governing bodies worked together. On this account, LMS has evolved from curriculum planning through staff development, resource allocation and marketing to a point where the aim is a coherent plan of development for each school. Convinced that co-operation between teachers and governors is necessary, she acknowledges the problem of governors who know little about teaching and have no meaningful contact with parents. She nevertheless remains optimistic that whole-school planning offers a way forward 'in the best interests of pupils'.

Alongside school development goes staff development, and Chapters 10 and 11 focus on funding for in-service training and the changes in teachers' professional roles.

In Chapter 11, Rob McBride argues that the notion that teaching is a 'rule-following activity' is implicit in recent policy initiatives and this represents the 'deprofessionalisation' of teaching. Contrasting the kind of staff development that seeks to enhance teachers' status as autonomous professionals, with INSET, he reviews the stages by which the curriculum has come to be viewed as 'delivered by management, rather than developed by teachers'. McBride argues that a teacher must inevitably use her own judgements in the classroom, and that these judgements should be 'guided by her membership of a professional body'. The gap that has been created by a 'deficit INSET', whereby experts identify teachers' needs or 'shortfalls' to be corrected by rules, is widened by the lack of an appropriate professional body to generate collective 'practical wisdom'. Drawing on data from four LEAs, he identifies a general lack of funding for and control over INSET budgets, whether INSET budgets are fragmented and devolved or held centrally in the LEA. DES requirements that LEAs may have money for INSET but are accountable to the DES, operate as a paradox. Long courses are no longer attracting funds and the demise of the LEA will be a disaster. Collaboration (although 'a slippery concept') between schools and (while they survive) LEAs, may offer a way forward. Theoretically, McBride draws parallels between what is happening to education and Hayek's (1960) concept of strong rules for a free market. However, teachers have not been given the opportunity to influence the strong laws 'expressed through the curriculum, testing and categorical funding'. He makes no apology for his 'negative' view of the present scenario; arguing that refusal to confront it amounts to suppression of the facts.

In Chapter 12, Hugh Busher takes a different line of argument to the same topic. He draws on data from three ethnographic studies of senior teachers in secondary schools. Reviewing the story of INSET, he notes how the dearth of funds, the lack of proper planning and the arbitrary nature of early provision has been through several stages of change culminating in a pattern of needs-based short courses geared to institutional requirements. For Busher, though, this is not the full story, as it ignores the growth in higher degrees and other qualifications, frequently financed by teachers themselves. His data are drawn from interviews with teachers, and take account of the similarities and differences in the way staff development is managed in different schools. Covering questions of leadership and of the membership, powers and administrative functions of the school's staff development committee, he shows how teachers worked within their particular situations. His conclusion is that the results cannot be conceptualised as one of 'deprofessionalisation'. The mistake lies in believing that professional teachers exist as 'loose associations of autonomous individuals'. His data suggest that a better definition is one of 'institutionalised professionals'.

In the final chapter, I pick up the themes of dilemmas and paradoxes, briefly reviewing the debate surrounding the view that managerial and educational approaches to schooling are fundamentally in conflict. Highlighting the conflicts over assessment, I argue that, in spite of the rhetoric, LMS has a pivotal role in locking 'self-management' into the mechanisms designed for increased central control. Far from 'closing the loop' in a rational, system of market competition and opportunity, tensions and paradoxes inherent in the system are devolved on to individuals and groups who experience them as stressful dilemmas and perversities.

Note

1. Circular 7/91 introduces the concept of the Potential Schools Budget (PSB). 85% of PSB must be delegated by 1 April 1993.

2 Local Management — The Kent Scheme

MIKE STEWART

The Background

This brief article sets out to review the impact of local management (LM) on schools in Kent. It is based on the findings by the author in the 147 schools for which he has responsibility in the South Kent area. The aim is to give readers an inside view of the Kent process of LM and perhaps indicate the way ahead for other authorities.

There are over 700 schools in Kent and the LEA is currently split into six Administrative Areas. These Areas are larger than many other Local Education Authorities (LEAs) and have responsibility for supporting all aspects of their schools' management.

Kent introduced LM as a pilot scheme to some schools in 1987. These schools received budgets to manage under restricted headings and in 1989 the scheme was extended to some 80 schools. Valuable lessons were learned from this pilot scheme which was so expanded that by April 1990 the South Kent Area had all 22 of its secondary schools and five of its primaries included within it. However, it should be pointed out that the funding was based on the schools' historic budgets.

The 1988 Education Reform Act

The changes that this Act has brought are well documented and they are not gone into in detail here. However, the key issues do need amplifying and the first has been referred to in the previous paragraph. The Kent pilot scheme, like many others in the country, was based on the schools' historic budgets. This meant that broadly speaking a school had a budget based on what it had, over time, negotiated and established for itself by the trading with, and persuading of, the LEA to recognise and provide extra resources for its individual needs. Of particular significance was the provision of 'discretionary staff' in response to special pleading. Evidence that 18 out of 22 of the Area's secondary schools lost money with the introduction of formula funding, reflects the loss of discretionary staffing in the change.

Discretionary staff were originally additional to entitlement and were provided for special reasons. With the passage of time they became accepted as the norm in that they were employed on the same basis as other staff. However, their existence, with the introduction of formula funding, caused the first of many problems for schools and local authority alike. The new distribution, based on actual pupil numbers, took little or no account of the previous cogent arguments used by headteachers to gain extra staffing. Indeed, with the introduction of formula funding, the LEA lost the pool of teachers available to it for distribution. The budget from which the pool was controlled had rested, historically, in the Area Office under the control of the personnel officer who also had responsibility for establishing and controlling the staffing establishment. In its management of the overall staffing budget, the local authority had the flexibility to deploy staff as it deemed appropriate. The Education Reform Act (1988), in introducing local management of schools, removed that role.

Funding is now an objective, formula-based, system and the local authority has to ensure that all schools are treated equally. There is no centrally controlled staffing budget that can allow for the provision of any staff to a school. Responsibility in this, as in other respects, has shifted out to the schools.

Kent's Formula

In the Kent scheme 80% of the money available has been devolved to schools, the bulk of it via a formula based on age-weighted pupil units (AWPU). The respective weightings are set out in Table 2.1.

Form 7, the DES statutory return, is completed by each school in January. The number in each age group is then multiplied, by the appropriate weighting, to determine the bulk of the funding for each institution. The weightings reflect the intention to avoid significantly affecting the established balances between sectors, such as between primary and secondary phases, in the financial year 1990/91. Kent is relatively unusual in providing a more generous level of funding for pupils studying two or more 'A' Level courses. This reflects the existence of grammar schools, as well as high schools and comprehensives, in the county structure. At the other end of the age spectrum,

TABLE 2.1 *The KCC allocation formula 1990/1991*

Pupil Number Related Funding

A. Age Weighted Pupil Units

Age Group	Weighting	Unit Funding £	Pupil Nos.
5+	1.4	1,091.70	
6+	1.0	779.78	
7+	1.0	779.78	
8+	1.0	779.78	
9+	1.0	779.78	
10+	1.0	779.78	
11+	1.5993	1,247.10	
12+	1.5993	1,247.10	
13+	1.5993	1,247.10	
14+	1.8044	1,406.99	
15+	1.8044	1,406.99	
Non A Level	1.9069	1,486.93	
A Level	2.5836	2,014.55	

Non Pupil Number Related Funding

Type	Unit	Unit Funding £	Number of Units
B. Premises Costs			
(i) Buildings Maintenance	Adjusted Floor Area (Square Metres)	0.3424	
(ii) Energy Costs	Electricity Target	0.0402	
	Gas Target	0.2618	
	Fuel Oil Target	0.0634	
(iii) Caretaking	Adjusted Floor Area (Square Metres)	4.13	
(iv) Grounds Maintenance	Gross Site Area (Hectares)	1562.29	

TABLE 2.1 (Continued)

C. Specific Factors

(i) Curriculum Protection Factor (Primary only)	Unweighted Roll		
(ii) Middle School Protection Factor	Unweighted Roll		70.00
(iii) Split Site Allowance	Defined		
(iv) Special Needs	Level 1 Assessment		220.00
	Level 2 Assessment		220.00
	Level 2 Assessment		600.00
(v) London Fringe Allowance (Qualifying Schools)	Weighted Roll	(P)	16.12
		(M)	16.95
		(S)	14.64
(vi) Social Priority (Qualifying Schools)	Weighted Roll	(P)	8.64
		(S)	13.49
(vii) Urban Allowance (Qualifying Schools)	Weighted Roll	(P)	31.79
		(S)	18.75
(viii) Rentals	Actual Cost		
D. Salary Adjustment Factor	Defined		
E. Safety Net Allocation	Defined		
F. Non-Domestic Rates	Rateable Value		

the 1.4 weighting of the youngest pupils was intended to encourage schools to take into their reception classes (Year R) non-statutory aged pupils (rising fives) if they wished, although only pupils who were five on or before 1st January 1990 were counted.

A sliding scale, the curriculum protection factor, was also an element of the formula. This was designed to support the smaller primaries, giving £18,000 to those with fewer than 101 on roll, tapering to £13,800 for schools with 125–200 pupils and then down to zero for schools with 300 or more.

Other factors were a middle schools' transitional protector, split-site allowances, urban, social, and London fringe allowances, and actual cost of rentals for premises used by schools for educational purposes, like parish halls and playing fields.

The final factor was devised through a special needs audit, which the DES recently agreed to allow to continue for the financial year 1991/92. An audit was carried out in each of the county's primary schools to measure the need of each child against known, objective criteria. By this means, the numbers of pupils needing additional funds to supplement their curriculum entitlement and ensure their needs were met, were identified. It requires a lot of work by both class teacher and support teacher to complete this process but it identifies and supports the need for a differentiated curriculum beyond the norm for recognised, individual pupils. The process is being extended to secondary schools, but in the financial year 1990/91 a roll-forward technique was used. This meant that, for secondary schools, the percentage of pupils with special needs that entered in year six from each of the feeder primaries was used to assess their special need percentage. This was then multiplied by the number on roll for years seven, eight and nine. It is regarded by the teachers involved as a useful and productive exercise and one that, although it requires many hours of work, allows for individual needs to be catered for. Cross-county moderation enhances its value.

The other major group identified for resource distribution contains the premises-related categories based on floor area, condition surveys, ground areas, types of contracts for maintenance of grounds, targets established for electricity, gas and oil, and the caretaking arrangements in use. Taken together, these ensure that actual factors related to the type of building are included in the formula and reflected in the level of resourcing.

The Impact

The impact of the LM funding arrangements has been dramatic. Evidence of this is still being gathered, but one of the most notable changes so far has been the new concern of educational managers to ensure that the resources available are used most effectively, reflecting the needs of the school. Many headteachers welcome this development, and I quote three typical responses from them:

> It has brought into focus for me the need to ensure that I monitor the spending of the school and that I spend wisely.

> I have found that I now look at what I buy rather than say, 'Because we had it last year, we must have it this'.

> The freedom to use my resources, although limited, is most welcome.

These serve to illustrate the beginning of the change appearing in the headteacher's role, a subject I shall be investigating further in due course. Suffice it to say here that headteachers are being forced away from their traditional role of Teacher towards that of Manager. Significantly, the amount of shift seems to depend on the relationship the headteachers have with their governors and the rest of their staff.

Another key player is the school secretary, whose job has undergone major changes to accommodate the financial monitoring process now required. Secretaries and headteachers have shouldered the burden which decentralisation has shifted on to schools.

The Balance

The ability to balance is the major part of the management's task in a school. It has been referred to already and the model in Figure 2.1 serves to illustrate the concept. It also indicates all the main budget headings. The source of income is the pupils, through their formula funded curriculum entitlement. For the school, curriculum entitlement means curriculum responsibility and the need to balance this against income. The crucial management function therefore rests on the ability to manipulate the resources allocated under each individual heading to ensure that pupils' needs (curriculum entitlement) are met and balance against the income available. It is, however, up to the school's management to ensure that the curriculum is actually delivered in an appropriate way to pupils. See Figure 2.1.

In Kent, training has been provided for all those involved in this process and the balance appears to be successful. However, it should be pointed out that balance applies also to the LEA at county level, where budgets must be balanced against resources and levels of service. The schools' budgets do not always appear to reflect the costs which, for example, apply nationally to teachers' pay and locally to premises.

The Governing Bodies

There can be no doubt that schools under the ERA are encouraged to take the management and decision-making role that controls their own destiny. This challenge is being met in South Kent through the Area Office working in partnership with the headteachers and governors of its schools. This shift of responsibility has perhaps been most pronounced in the change in the role of governors who could have been seen as a rubber-stamping body but who are now very much in the forefront of the education, planning and management scene. To respond to the demand on their time and expertise, many governors have organised themselves into committees or sub-groups. Some of these have been established through necessity, for example to meet the requirements of the disciplinary and grievance procedure which requires two panels. One is to process the initial complaint and the other is to hear the

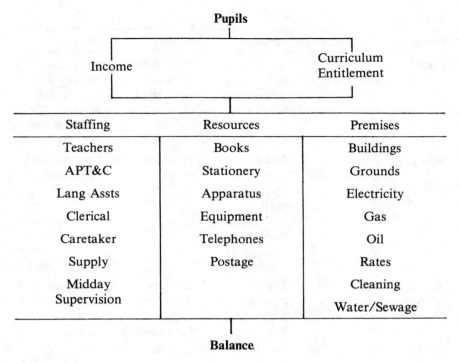

FIGURE 2.1

appeal. Others are established as a result of the need to ensure that the responsibilities now devolved to schools are covered. Table 2.2 illustrates, in a summative form, some of the responsibilities of each sub-group and the scope and depth of the governors' role.

Although Kent has, at the time of writing this article (January 1991), some 324 schools (out of 724) fully in LM, all the schools in the authority are encouraged to treat themselves as though they are fully LM. The success of this must be measured by the fact that an additional 202 schools wished to join the scheme in September 1990 rather than wait for a later date. However, the DES rejected such a proposal and now all schools, except for the Specials, will become full participants of the scheme from April 1991.

Obviously there has been much attention to the budgetary process in the schools of the LEA and this has perhaps been more significant in Kent than elsewhere. Kent has delegated to its schools almost complete autonomy in terms of budgetary controls, with the allocation via a formula for all the budgets outlined in the lower boxes of the 'Balance' model in Figure 2.1.

TABLE 2.2

Functions	Curriculum	People	Budget	Buildings
Make	Set up Resource Timetable Room	Identify posts Advertising Appropriate funding	Prioritise How much to what heading	Decide priorities authorising works establishing funding
Maintain	Staff availability Resources	Stability of staff INSET Staff Development Scene of belonging/ ownership	How and who runs it	Continuous upkeeping
Manage	Best use of time and resources	Decide responsibilities Conditions of Service	Delegate decisions Responsibility for spending	Contract management Health and Safety
Modify	Effect change as needed Respond to Gov directives ERA and Nat Curric	Changes Subject reviews Analysing and improving	Identify a process and person for this	Adapting premises, and keeping up with legislation
Monitor	Ensure Curric delivery Testing, SAT's and records of achievement	Appraisal Scrutinise exam results Know pupils and staff	Controlling ensuring management action is taken as appropriate	Regular reviewing
Market	Dissemination of information to those that need it	Attract the best staff Advertising Publish pupil and staff success	Communicate information to the people who need it	Lettings and establish a co-operative image

The main source of income to a school is via the LEA's formula which is based on the structure shown in Table 2.1 and is used to distribute all the Authority's aggregated schools budget. The element retained centrally by Kent was among the lowest in the country. Centrally held funds meet the cost of the statutory services of the LEA and its administrative function.

The Future

It is now very difficult to predict with any confidence the future in education as there is so much uncertainty and change. LM has brought one of the most fundamental changes. It has given responsibility to schools at the point of greatest contact between the client and the provider of the service. This creates challenges for an LEA, and the budget for Kent in the financial year of 1991/92 reflects some of these. However, the ability of schools to determine their own destiny at a local level would seem generally welcome. The level at which schools are funded and the degree of control they have are the two most contentious issues. LM has brought much freedom and greater control to schools and, in 1992 and 1993, will undoubtedly bring more. Grant maintained (GM) status is now firmly on the agenda and is perceived by some as an extension of LM, although it may lead to the demise of LEAs as they are currently recognised. Its funding and impact on LEAs is still far from clear. However, it is the author's view that it should not be GM at the expense of all schools that remain in an LEA, nor should the pupils receiving their education in one school suffer at the expense of another.

Other aspects of school life will also change. Most noticeably perhaps will be their ability to enter the open marketplace for services they require. Forward-looking schools are already addressing this issue and are beginning to try to provide services to other schools. Each school is unique and as such has its own set of circumstances, but under LM the need for the management of the school to recognise these and to capitalise on them would seem crucial to survival. The need for curriculum planning and school development plans that allow for a plan of the development of the whole school, along with budget implications, is growing and is becoming an increasingly important tool for school management.

Budgets for LEAs are being set as this article is being written (January 1991), and changes will be brought to schools to reflect the new levels of funding. One approach is for Kent to move towards using its weightings to reflect a common policy for post-16 education. Other changes are likely to be in the weighting for the Year R (reception) pupils and the curriculum protection weighting. The use of such weightings to reflect county policy is an area that could be extensively debated. The rationale of using such weightings to reflect key stages of the national curriculum is another area for possible debate, as is the need to maintain levels of funding to various types of schools, as has been indicated above. Additional minor changes may also occur, such as the proposed implementation of processes for calculating a split-site allowance.

Ultimately, the money available to fund each AWPU, in all authorities, is intimately linked to the overall size of the Authority's budget and is therefore directly connected to the level of community charge that a county is prepared to accept.

Finally, the Education Reform Act (1988) is encouraging schools to take on a more businesslike image and is certainly a major incentive for schools to become more responsive to their customers. Indeed, regardless of who these customers are perceived to be, the vast majority of schools in the author's area of Kent appear to be responding positively to this challenge. Many schools welcome the changes LM has brought and the benefits to the ultimate customer, the pupil. It would appear to be going extremely well in the Area's schools, although this has not been achieved without some problems not least of which has been the increase of workloads for those responsible for its implementation. There has been much planning in the schools and the times are both exciting and challenging for school management. LM will allow schools to bring these plans to fruition to the benefit of all the pupils in the educational system.

3 The Policy Implications of LMS[1]

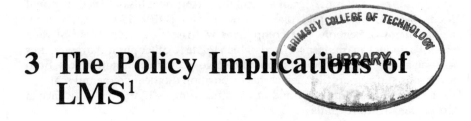

MARGARET MADEN

> Local management of schools presents a major challenge and a major opportunity for the education service. The introduction of needs-based funding and the delegation of financial and managerial responsibilities to governing bodies are key elements in the Government's overall policy to improve the quality of teaching and learning in schools. Local management is concerned with far more than budgeting and accounting procedures. Effective schemes of local management will enable governing bodies and head teachers to plan their use of resources — including their most valuable resource, their staff — to maximum effect in accordance with their own needs and priorities, and to make schools more responsive to their clients — parent, pupils, the local community and employers.
> DES (1988a: General Principles, Para 9)

There are several objectives and, indeed, assumptions in this extract which need to be unpicked and, perhaps, scrutinised and investigated by researchers.

Examples of the questions which need to be asked might be:

- In what way is formula funding 'needs-based'?
- In what way (or ways) will local management of schools (LMS) lead to an improvement in the 'quality of teaching and learning in schools'?
- How will governing bodies and headteachers be enabled to 'plan their use of resources' — and where is the LEA in all of this?
- Will LMS 'make schools more responsive to their clients' who, we are told, comprise 'parents, pupils, the local community and employers'?

The Needs-based Formula

In the first place, a needs-based formula has to articulate a range of educational needs with money. The LMS formula assumes that at least 75% of a school's need is determined simply by numbers of pupils weighted by age.

21

In this sense, it is the age of a pupil that determines his or her educational need. Indeed, we are told that in the circular (DES, 1991) on the local management of schools, this component will rise to at least 80%[2] of each school's budget share. Hence, needs which relate to other pupil characteristics — such as special educational needs and socio-economic circumstances, or to a school's staffing profile such as age or position on the incremental scale, or to the age and condition of buildings and furniture — have no significance in the current LMS formula.

It would therefore be a valuable research exercise to investigate a taxonomy of needs against which the current LMS formula rules could be tested.

Improving the Quality of Teaching and Learning

Secondly, it is, indeed, vital that a radical move to formula funding and to local management at school level should lead to an improvement in the quality of teaching and learning. But this too cannot be simply assumed. It has to be tested. Case studies of individual schools which showed how they were using their increased powers, including the allocation of large budgets, would be illuminating.

However, the connection between educational quality and the allocation of resources is notoriously difficult to establish. The decision to switch resources from staffing or premises maintenance to books and materials, or vice versa, *may* lead to an improvement in educational quality but, again, this cannot simply be assumed. We first need to be clear about the nature of improved teaching and learning. Will this be simply *outcomes* measured in terms of national curriculum assessment scores together with, for secondary schools, examination results? Such measures would take no account of measures of input such as pupils' previous attainment or levels of family support. Neither would they reckon with the nature of *process* factors such as class size and pupil – teacher ratios, the unit of resource available in different classes or departments, or the availability of extra-curricular activities and support.

How far do process factors and characteristics represent, in themselves, important outcomes as far as pupils are concerned? Inspectors, after all, have usually concentrated their observations and 'quality audit' work on process rather than output or 'results' when deciding whether or not a school is good, less good or plain awful.

Will inspectors now need to investigate the relationship between resource allocation management decisions and educational quality? More to the point, are they equipped to do so?

An alternative view is implicit in the 'educational marketplace' concept. This seems to recommend a simpler and far cheaper method of determining quality: the parents, as consumers, decide quality by the choices they exercise. Hence, the reasoning goes, popular schools are good schools just as popular television programmes are good — or so we are led to believe.

Managerial Abilities, Planning and the Budget

The third area for scrutiny needs to question how far the extent to which LMS enables governors and heads to plan their use of resources depends on the managerial abilities of the people concerned as well as on the nature of the school's historic budget.

Managerial abilities are variable and depend, to an extent, on the quality of training provided and the reliability and quality of information available. Both these are, in large part, dependent on the local authority. So we must ask how effective is the training provided by LEAs? How reliable or helpful, or even understandable, are the financial reports they provide? Moving from macro-reports across a large system to detailed school by school financial reports represents a massive challenge and the technical complexity of this should not be underestimated.

In short, individual schools cannot plan effectively if the data is unreliable.

Furthermore, HM Inspectorate recently observed that a major problem in schools is that of 'vestigial management skills'. This suggests that moving from a point where effective management has been concerned mainly with producing a workable timetable to one where the management of, often, a £1 million budget and quite complex personnel issues is challenging indeed. We need to know how it is all working.

What, for example, happens to headteachers and other professionals when planning for more than a term is required — and when careful budgeting has to be linked to educational and curricular planning? Even more crucially, what *is* the nature of the head's role in relation to the governing body?

For several years to come, the other main constraint or opportunity for schools and their planning capacity will be the difference between the results of formula funding and the nature of their historic budgets. Those schools which are losers rather than winners in the serendipity of formula funding, particularly where the situation is worsened by falling rolls, will have quite restricted planning options. With 75–80% of a school's expenditure taken by staffing costs, if a school's loss is of the order of £20,000 or more then reducing staff by one or two is the obvious option.

Alternatively — or as well — schools may decide to reduce the non-contact time of teachers either generally or through the increasing practice of using permanent staff to cover the classes of absent colleagues. Will such decisions be monitored, and by whom? How will we know if such practices lead to an improvement in the quality of teaching and learning?

Responding to Clients

The fourth point covers those general principles underlying LMS which suggest that schools will become 'more responsive to their clients — parents, pupils, the local community and employers'. There is no doubt that this represents the major potential strength of LMS. However, just as the other principles or assertions need to be tested, so does this. Most obviously there is a real problem in assuming a coherent set of expectations and needs among the four categories of clients listed.

An open enrolment policy places the parent as the major, most powerful client. For it is the cumulative parent choice of school that determines the school's budget and, therefore, to a large extent, its capacity to provide an effective and broadly based education. However, this may also obscure one of the most damaging assumptions of the Education Reform Act (1988). In de-coupling the parent and teacher it replaces the notion of partnership and shared responsibility by a model where the parent is the 'client' and the teacher, presumably, the 'contractor'.

This raises a number of new questions. For example, what happens if the teachers believe that parents' expectations are inappropriate — perhaps too narrow or perhaps too extensive? What happens if the local community, whoever this is meant to include, is at odds with parental or local employer interests? Do we not need to know more about this multi-client group and their respective expectations? Likewise, in what ways does the locally managed school become more responsive to these different stakeholders?

In giving marketing a higher profile, will the deeper issues of educational quality and minority interests, whether they be those of ethnic groups or children with special needs, be obscured?

The Role of the LEA

My final area of concern, to which the general principles of Circular 7/88 (DES 1988a) make no reference, is the role of the LEA.

Increasing pressure emerges week by week for LEAs to divest themselves of central support services — legal, personnel, financial, advisory, as well as those more directly affecting particular schools and groups; centres for pupils who are emotionally and behaviourally disturbed, museum and library services, residential centres, education psychologists and so on.

It is clear that schools need more money for efficient and effective management as well as for books, materials and, of course, staff. Whether this should or could come from greedy, bureaucratic local authorities is another matter. First of all, the 3–4% spent on central administration would not actually result in any kind of 'at a stroke' solution for schools. Secondly, the unit costs of necessary, if rather boring, support services would rise if their budgets were simply delegated.

Most LEA services represent value for money, although the discipline, arising from LMS, of having to make public and scrutinise LEA discretionary exceptions (held back from schools) is entirely healthy.

Research is needed into the impact of delegation on schools — what happens to the cost, efficiency and quality of services: legal, payroll, the administration of staff appointments, buildings maintenance — and the rest — when these functions and their budgets are delegated on an age-weighted pupil formula? This is probably why the Coopers & Lybrand (1988) initial report on LMS warned that LMS would not be cheap. In this context, we also need to ask what the relationship is between such delegation and notions of equity or need.

Apart from further delegation of both money and powers, there is a great deal that has to be done by the LEA. I favour a 'leaner and meaner' LEA, but I do not favour the view that LMS means either 'UDI' on the part of schools or the end of the LEA. Rather, a much misunderstood paradox of delegation is that a stronger, not weaker, monitoring and quality control function is needed at the centre. The impact and implications of LMS need to be evaluated and reported on.

The simple notion of parental choice of school, based largely on historic reputation and unweighted assessment scores, needs to be qualified and attenuated by clear LEA reporting on educational quality and the management decisions of headteachers and governors.

A clear agenda for evaluation and research is emerging, some of which needs to be conducted by outside consultants. I have tried to suggest an agenda for researchers to engage in systematic enquiry on projects designed to enlighten us all on the full consequences of LMS for education.

Notes

1. This is an edited version of a talk given to a BERA/LMS Regional Conference at Derbyshire College of Higher Education on 1st November, 1990.
2. Confirmed in December, 1990.

4 A View from the Front

ROBERT McGOVERN

This paper attempts to explore the hopes, doubts and fears surrounding the implementation of local management of schools (LMS) in an 8–12 middle school. It reflects upon the debate in governors' meetings and staffrooms, and questions the assumption that financial delegation will improve the quality of teaching and learning in our schools.

In the months leading up to the September 1989 deadline for the submission of Local Education Authority (LEA) schemes to the Department of Education and Science (DES), governors, headteachers and teachers were forming their own opinions of the impact of LMS on their school and their community. In the early stages LMS seemed to offer the sort of challenge and responsibility most headteachers and governors had been waiting many years for — financial independence from the LEA, a chance to manage the school budget and to prioritise spending for themselves. As an elected teacher governor I was in an ideal position to be both spectator and participant in a process that, as it unfolded, left many early enthusiasts feeling vulnerable and sceptical about the promised benefits.

Of circular 7/88 (DES, 1988a), Kenneth Baker announced:

> Local management is essentially concerned with the quality of education. Schools will be free to deploy resources to their own needs and priorities . . . Headteachers will have powers to match their responsibilities. Local management will mean better education. (DES, 1988b)

Among my colleagues (both teachers and governors) there was considerable support for the principle of delegation. Many teachers and headteachers had found themselves at odds with the LEA at some time. The supposed cost, size and remoteness of most educational administration from the point of delivery — classrooms — made it an easy target. Local management would provide real power for headteachers, allowing them much greater freedom to allocate resources. Removing power from the LEA would curb political excesses and would result in the eventual demise of the educational administrator — the butt of many staffroom jokes.

As the meetings proceeded and the LEA consultation documents filtered through, the true reality of the application of local management began to dawn on us. The extent of the partnership which existed between members and officers of the LEA and schools became more apparent. For the first time many governors and teachers were beginning to realise the true extent of the delegated powers and were beginning to question their ability to manage without continued support from the local authority.

In the early stages, discussion at governors' meetings stressed the advantages. Most governors saw the school gaining. It was expected that there would be virement; that savings would be made by using local suppliers and tradesmen, and that these savings would be used to enhance staffing or to make a start on the long overdue redecoration or refurnishing programme.

Statements prepared for governors by the LEA put this into perspective. Many of my fellow governors were shocked to discover that staffing costs accounted for 75% or more of spending. There was further concern when it was realised that earlier legislation had resulted in cleaning and grounds maintenance being provided by the Direct Services Organisation which had won the county contract — most for a minimum number of years and with little likelihood of change. The great *brouhaha* that welcomed delegation seemed to be subsiding into feelings of confusion, disappointment and a growing realisation that schools and governors had been sold something which offered them little real power in return for a lot more work. The supposed move from a centrally controlled and determined budget to the general principle and purpose of LMS, which was to enable schools and governors to allocate resources according to their own needs and priorities, was beginning to look a sham.

I had worked with many of my fellow governors for more than five years. In that time they had shown themselves to be hard working and conscientious. Just a glance at the minutes of meetings for the past five years indicated the extent of the reforms and the volume of business they had dealt with: LEA policies on the curriculum; personal and social education; multiracial and equal opportunities statements; sex education; special educational needs. DES originated statements regarding their role and powers; the composition of governing bodies; annual meetings with parents; the introduction of the national curriculum; charging policies; school hours. On top of this, the most crucial job of all, their involvement in the day-to-day running of the school and ensuring the quality of education which every child deserves. Most had come to terms with the volume of paperwork and were thankful when the LEA provided a dictionary of useful acronyms! But many were finding it difficult to devote enough time to the extra meetings and subcommittees created to deal with the volume of business. Some governors resigned, others made clear their intention not to serve again.

A combination of the pressure of time and the constant articulation of figures from balance sheets indicated that we were becoming obsessed by managerialism. Strenuous efforts were being made to understand systems of accounting and finance, but little was done to relate this to the quality of teaching and learning in the school. We spent one very long winter evening discussing the minutia of delegation of powers of expenditure, only to discover (when we came to vote on a proposal which would have effectively harnessed the headteacher to a subcommittee for permission to spend on all but essential stock) that, perhaps already tired by such discussion, we had not achieved a quorum! It was a salutory lesson for us all.

The School Development Plan

The LEA, I am sure, recognised the widening gulf between governors' and teachers' ideas about LMS and sought to place the financial delegation within an overall management plan for the school. The school development plan (SDP) was introduced in the spring. It was to act as a focus for all aspects of planning in the school, linking financial planning with curriculum aims and plans, staff development plans, in-service training (INSET) needs and priorities, deployment of staff, community involvement and forward planning. The plan required schools to ask four fundamental questions:

- Where is our school now?
- What changes do we need to make?
- How shall we manage these over the next few years?
- How will we know whether we have managed the changes successfully?
(See Hargreaves et al., 1989b.)

The questions seemed simple enough. Perhaps it was assumed that many schools had been guided by similar management principles in the past and would respond quickly and easily. The reality was that many headteachers and senior staff threw up their hands in horror. At a time when every available moment was devoted to implementing the national curriculum and its associated assessment and record-keeping, we were now being asked to wrap our very limited financial powers around a more comprehensive development plan.

It was, of course, right that we should do so. The LEA acted swiftly and generously to provide the necessary information and support. They even provided supply cover for headteachers in primary schools with large teaching commitments. However, it all seemed so rushed that the major gains of such a plan — consultation, consensus, agreement of aims and objectives, were not so clearly articulated when the plan had to be produced in a very short time and in the context of so many other changes.

In the long term I am sure that a mandatory SDP will prove to be the most useful exercise in school management. It certainly puts the financial management into perspective — as merely supporting the curriculum and the quality of provision for the children.

Savings

The questions, or section headings, in the SDP gave the school and its governors the chance to decide their own objectives and a timetable for meeting them. True financial delegation would give them the power, by cost-saving and virement, to bring those changes about.

It became obvious that for LMS to be successful and worthwhile there would have to be virement of at least 2% from *all* budget headings to supplies and services every year. Only in this way could greater autonomy and creative management be achieved. Anything less than 2% would leave schools with much the same as before — a capitation allowance straining to cope with the demands of the curriculum, largely spent on consumable items. Governors were aware (some for the first time) that much more money would be needed if the refurnishing and remodelling (identified as a priority in the development plan) were to become a reality. Scrutiny of the balance sheets cast doubt in many minds that such savings could be made. Few teachers or governors were reassured by Kenneth Baker's exhortations. One effect of the Government's insistence that LMS would bring about improvements, although I am sure unintended, was to make governors more aware of the underfunding of school building projects over the last ten years and the lack of investment in books and equipment to meet the needs of the national curriculum.

The introduction of LMS has opened up school financing to greater, and more easily understood, public scrutiny. Many governors, headteachers and teachers now fear that LMS will not automatically enlarge school budgets. It is becoming clear that there will be winners and losers. It is not yet known who they will be, or how the gains in one school will compare with the enforced budget deficit in another. It might be safer to hope for funding at present levels — but why, then, all of the extra work and worry? One thing is certain, this greater awareness of how (badly) schools are financed has contributed to the general consensus that education is underfunded, and added weight to the growing demands for a change in government policy.

The Hopes and Fears

The weeks spent preparing the budget and the SDP seemed to be filled with meetings, discussions with senior colleagues, and the inevitable final checks with a calculator. The headteacher groaned with every digit, disbelieving the enthusiasm of colleagues in pilot schools. So much time and effort had been spent preparing a budget which might provide a baseline for the future, but provided no real opportunities in the current financial year. Full delegation was still one or two years away and until that time there was no point worrying about underspends or overspends. This process was to prove more useful to the LEA in raising awareness; revealing problems and training headteachers and school secretaries. In the coming financial year there would be no direct financial benefit to individual schools.

Clerical Support

The one role which was to be changed most radically by the introduction of LMS was that of the school secretary or clerk. Not surprisingly many secretaries felt undervalued. Traditionally, secretaries in primary schools have always been regarded as 'the face of the school'. In addition to the administrative and clerical work of the school most secretaries give generously of their time to the many other tasks which school life presents. As so often happens, this loyalty and dedication fell prey to LMS and many secretaries became overworked, underpaid victims. Most are paid for only a proportion of the year. In a large primary school the secretary might be paid for 27.5 hours per week. She can therefore expect to earn a little more than £5,000 p.a. The introduction of LMS has extended their role to include financial controller and personal assistant. Most will become computer literate. All earn less than half the salary of the youngest teacher. Their goodwill is central to the success of LMS. More importantly, it is their skills which will enable headteachers to concentrate on professional issues — improving the quality of teaching and learning. It became obvious as the year went on that some way must be found to reward them. Even on the basis of a simple cost comparison (have I been touched by the message of LMS?) it makes sense. A headteacher in an average primary school will earn £20,000. If only one hour each day is spent on routine LMS issues (a modest estimate) the direct cost to the school is £20,000 ÷ 1,265 (contract hours) × 195 (school days) = £3,083 p.a. The indirect costs are immeasurable. The same work done by a school secretary would cost less than £1,000 p.a. Striking a balance between the role of the headteacher as manager of the whole SDP, or simply as budget/site manager, will be difficult in primary schools unless the role of the school secretary in LMS is recognised and rewarded.

Teaching Staff

Hopes and fears of, and for, teaching staff fall into three main areas: (1) the changing role of the headteacher; (2) the demands made upon teachers by LMS; (3) the management of teachers. It has to be said that not all headteachers welcome the changes which LMS imposes on them. In many primary schools, particularly the smaller schools, the role of the head has been that of a teacher who manages. Most see this as the only way to implement curriculum change, support staff and maintain the close links with parents and children which the community has come to associate with primary schools. There are certain, obvious, executive and administrative tasks that only a headteacher can perform. Teachers and governors would not question that, and most headteachers are appointed because they show a certain aptitude or ability to be able to balance those various demands of headship. What must be called into question is any system which diverts headteachers of primary schools from the more familiar role of the teacher who manages, and imposes a style of management which limits the time they have available for teaching and interacting with pupils and staff. This is a major area of concern for schools. Similarly, many teachers would not wish to become involved in financial management and there is clearly resentment that incentive allowances (up to allowance 'E' in the secondary sector) are being used for this purpose. The role of the teacher is clear (DES, 1987c) — direct teaching; planning; preparing and evaluating courses and lessons; assessing, testing and recording the development, progress and attainment of pupils. Any distraction from this inevitably means less time teaching pupils. Incentive allowances paid to teachers for administering the financial aspects of delegation clearly undermine the original intention that they should be awarded for outstanding classroom performance, curriculum leadership or evaluating the standards of teaching and learning — another sickening blow to the morale of dedicated class teachers who feel that their work with the children continues to be undervalued.

A further cause for concern is the new relationship between the individual teacher and his or her employer. The Education Reform Act (1988) placed the power of hire and fire firmly with governing bodies. Under the Act, the LEA is no longer able to set a staff complement for a school. Governors will be able to treat teachers as they do any other resource. The implications of this change have fuelled considerable debate and anxiety in staffrooms. Few teachers seriously believe that governors would engage in a witch-hunt and most accept that they are reasonably well protected by statutory provisions. However, there remains considerable anxiety about overstaffing and whether this would result in redeployment or compulsory redundancy. This fear is justified.

Falling rolls have forced many LEAs, schools, governors and teachers to cope with overstaffing and voluntary redeployment or retirement. Fair and consistent LEA management of this problem, combined with Trade Union agreements have, in the majority of cases, resulted in voluntary or compulsory redeployment to the satisfaction of all involved. Many schools were left overstaffed until reasonable agreement could be reached. This will no longer be the case. Individual schools will simply be unable to afford to be overstaffed. Schools, in the same authority, advertising vacancies will be under no obligation to accept redeployed staff. This will result in uncertainty, low morale and an unseemly scramble for jobs in those schools which appear to be successful in attracting pupils and money. For those unfortunate governors who have to manage the schools which lose out it will be like driving a bus down hill with faulty brakes — staff and pupils will not want to wait and see if the bus stops short of disaster — they'll jump off before the driver finally loses control! In such schools considerable time and effort will be spent on survival. The help and support of the LEA will not be able to compensate for the reality of a budget deficit. Children will suffer.

The School and the Community

The national curriculum requires that the themes of economic and industrial awareness should permeate the curriculum. The argument seems to be that if we are preparing children for life in the enterprise culture, and their schools are to be run along business lines, there should be some acknowledge-ment of it in the primary school curriculum. This theme has become well established in the national curriculum long before documents relating to the creative arts (one of the most powerful vehicles for teaching young children) are even published. In truth this acknowledgement of economic and industrial awareness is more likely to provide funds for the butterfly garden or pond. There were many suggestions for curriculum-led fund-raising, many of which sought donations from local retailers or manufacturers. Many primary schools will use local shops and small businesses as their starting points and by so doing they will undoubtedly enhance the children's learning and the role of the school in the community. They will rarely reach larger retailers or companies (even if they do, the record of the Government in trying to persuade industry to fund city technical colleges (CTCs) provides little incentive) and will find that the one-off donation is about as much as most small businesses can afford. The meagre sums involved made me feel uncomfortable about asking for help — a real lesson in economic and industrial awareness!

Staff and governors are always enthusiastic about fund-raising. The idea of getting something for nothing has immediate appeal. Rarely, in my experience, is this the case. Most fund-raising requires considerable time and effort from professional staff, and their priorities are more likely to conflict with those who would simply make money. Most teachers will give up their own time if they feel that the event moves the school closer to the parents and children. It is the quality of the relationship which is enhanced, not the school funds. British primary schools are not seen as the Alma Mater. It is one service which parents still expect to be provided free of charge. Few professionals involved would disagree. Some would go further and expect levels of funding which help to close the gaps and alleviate social disadvantage. Within such well established principles, most teachers would only accept fund-raising if it enhanced spending beyond an acceptable baseline for all children. The test for any revenue-raising scheme must surely be the effects on the pupils and whether the schemes are consistent with the aims of the school. Primary teachers are well aware that one way to make money (and a lot of it!) would be to exploit the sweet and toy market. So far common sense has prevailed (not so in all secondary schools) and the signs are that most teachers and governors understand the difference between inefficient begging and fund-raising.

In spite of this there remained in the minds of some governors and teachers resentment that the LEA would have the upper hand in determining the level of compensation schools should receive as a result of community use. Adult education, youth and community activities would make considerable demands on energy and cleaning costs. They might even interfere with more lucrative lettings. Fortunately, such conflict is unlikely to occur. By the end of the year it became clear that the LEA would do all that it could to preserve and encourage traditional community use. Under the formula LEAs can make separate provision to schools to cover community use as long as it does not come from the general schools' budget. Every school was compensated for community use. What was not immediately apparent was whether the sums involved related to actual use, or whether it was calculated as a percentage of the total budget. If the latter, then some of the most effective community schools could be disadvantaged — another example of winners and losers under formula funding.

'D Evolution Day' and Beyond

Recent legislation has signalled a strong desire to weaken the influence of the LEAs: the removal of the polytechnics from local authority control; open enrolment; CTCs; grant maintained status by 'opting out'; the national curriculum, and more recently local management of schools. There is no mistaking the intentions of this government. LMS is seen as one more step along the way to all schools becoming grant maintained by 'opting out'. Few of my colleagues, teachers or governors want this. By the end of the consultation process and the preparation of the first budget sheet, most governors were acutely aware of the need to maintain a close partnership with the LEA. Few teachers could see worthwhile financial benefits accruing to their schools and many felt much more vulnerable and uncertain about the future. Many headteachers, who had been influenced by reports from pilot schools in other authorities, could not understand the enthusiasm of their colleagues — an indication of the urgent need for formal evaluation and research. Many are worried about the duties and responsibilities LMS has imposed on an already difficult job. Few people who have regular daily contact with primary schools see the introduction of LMS as offering the considerable benefits referred to by the Secretary of State. As a way of encouraging greater numbers of schools to 'opt out' the government has recently announced that any school, regardless of size, can now ballot parents. I would expect most schools to remain in LEA control, governed and managed by those who would prefer to see all schools properly funded, rather than having to compromise their vision of what a state education system should be providing by competing for funds or pupils in an uncertain marketplace.

5 'Doing What Should Come Naturally': An Exploration of LMS in One Secondary School[1]

RICHARD BOWE and STEPHEN BALL

Introduction

In looking at the impact of the 1988 Educational Reform Act (ERA), we want to move away from seeing policy as the imposition of a fixed piece of legislation and explore the view that policy is a continual process which requires analyses sensitive to both its historical and dialectical dimensions. The historical dimension is as evident in the changing languages of the school with the new talk of budgeting, educational audits, cost-effectiveness, 'on costs', etc., as it is in the changing structures and processes of management. In addition the steady 'drip feed' of circulars and pronouncements from ministers and the Department of Education and Science (DES), provides further possibilities for continually shifting the available policy interpretations. The dialectical dimension requires us to recognise that the processes of policy change, at national, local, school and classroom level, may have significant implications for each other and may be more or less 'loosely coupled' over time.

In a recent paper on the national curriculum we tried to develop this notion of policy as process, conceptually, by suggesting that it is helpful to see policy, analytically, as multifaceted, with interrelated policy arenas each containing the facets of intended policy, actual policy and policy-in-use (Ball & Bowe, 1990). It is not only a question of analysing these facets of policy but also the gaps, and the relationships between them, as they shift over time. In the case of LMS we begin by trying to clarify the government's policy intentions, with regard to schools as institutions. This is a necessary forerunner because the legislation itself, the actual policy, is written in a technical-bureaucratic language. We then explore the micro-political dimension, i.e. the way in which government policy, in all its complexity, finds a presence within one school. The purpose is to try and grasp both the extent and the way in which LMS has entered the discourses of schooling and how the institutional practices may be changing as a consequence.

For the government, LMS is firmly embedded within an ERA that is to be seen 'as a piece'. The varying aspects of the Act are intended to bring about changes in the nature of schooling that draw the primary and secondary sector of the educational system closer to particular strands of Tory thinking. (We concentrate upon the secondary sector and accept that while the two sectors may well have some aspects in common, there are significant differences between them.) This provides us with a series of questions:

What does the ERA, market-based view of education actually involve and how does the government intend to make the 'connection' between the market and the institutional practices of the schools? How, in crude terms, is the climate set by the market intended to affect the micro climates of the schools? This leads us to ask how the Act in general and LMS in particular, anticipate a new culture of management within 'schools as enterprises' and how the new institutional practices of schooling are intended to change the relationships between schools and the state (local and national), parents, governors and employers?

LMS and the school as an enterprise

Unlike the development of the national curriculum, LMS has no roots in the educational world. Its ideological genealogy derives, partly, from nineteenth-century *laissez-faire* politics and the more recent writings of neo-liberal economists such as Hayek (1976) and Friedman (1980), and partly from more recent developments in organisational theory (Caldwell & Spinks, 1988: 3–25). To this extent it is not directly concerned with matters of pedagogy, theories of learning or questions about assessment. Rather, LMS reflects a strand in Tory thinking that wishes to alter significantly the relationship between the State, social policy provision and institutional management. Put simply, it seeks to privilege 'market mechanisms' over and above a state co-ordinated and managed system.

For neo-liberals, such as Hayek and Friedman, the market solution to the planning and delivery of education rests on two premises. Firstly, the belief that decentralised markets maximise creative entrepreneurship through the drive for profit — and are thus better for coping with rapid social and technological change — and with uncertainty:

Through the pursuit of selfish aims the individual will usually lead himself to serve the general interest, the collective actions of organized groups are almost invariably contrary to the general interest. (Hayek, 1976: 138)

This may not produce equality, indeed that would be counter-productive in market terms, but it is not seen to be unfair. Thus the market will provide a natural economic order and even the poorest should benefit from the progress of the society as a whole.

Secondly, freedom of choice can be only fully achieved in the marketplace as against the coercion of monopolistic state provision. The imposition of taxation to fund state provision is unfavourably contrasted with the opportunity to dispose of one's own income:

An essential part of economic freedom is freedom to choose how to use our income; how much to spend on ourselves and on what items . . . we choose in the light of our own needs and desires. (Friedman, 1980: 89)

The 1988 ERA realises these central premises by seeking to establish the mechanisms and conditions for a market in education (see Ball, 1990). Its operation is to rest on five main, interrelated factors: (1) *choice* via 'open enrolment'; (2) *diversity* via the extension of the current choice of schools; (3) *competition* via the diversity of schools competing to be 'chosen' by parents, thus moving control of education away from the producers (teachers) and towards the consumers ('parents, pupils, the local community and employers') (4) per capita *funding* to connect the 'product' to market forces, with individual school funding being primarily determined by student numbers (each student enrolled bringing a fixed sum to the school enabling parental views of the comparative performances of different schools to have a direct financial consequence); and (5) *organisation*, requiring schools to take direct control of their individual budgets, thus linking the new funding system to the internal school decision making, that is by connecting the management of the school directly to market forces.

The key question posed for schools by the Act is not simply how cost-effective is the running of the school but: how cost-effectively are you processing students in line with the national curriculum? Schools are encouraged to balance their budgets and generate the maximum income to enhance the product. The educational process becomes the production process, teachers are producers, parents are consumers, knowledge becomes a commodity and the educated student the product, with a minimum specification laid down by the national curriculum. It is further asserted that a budget-conscious system of organisational decision making will raise educational standards. Under LMS it is hoped this process, operating at an institutional level, will be driven by the educational market which effectively charges the schools with 'managing their own salvation'. Thus the government's ideological commitment to market forces is combined with a critique of existing institutional practices in a way that privileges organisational and managerial concerns. It is not simply a matter of 'linking' the market to individual schools but of setting out to transform institutional forms of educational provision, in particular the notion of a state 'system'. Briefly, there is, in New Right thinking, a strong belief that a state run educational system produces systemic dependency (schools dependent upon 'the system'), complacency (an unresponsiveness to the demands of society), bureaucracy (inititives for change hampered by 'red tape'), and 'protectionism' (educational quality judged by the 'professionals', whose central concerns may not be in the national or the consumers interests). The argument then follows that such tendencies can be eradicated only if spending is devolved to schools as individual enterprises required to respond to some form of educational market. For the government, the essence of LMS is buried within the move to market driven funding. This encourages schools to enter a new era of self-help, entrepreneurialism, cost-effectiveness and consumerism.

The promotion of *self-determination* is intended to erode any sense of an educational 'system' and replace it with a market-driven, free-floating, diverse set of enterprises (schools), charged with delivering products (schooled persons) with a minimum quality specification (the skills and knowledge of the national curriculum). The management of change is to rest with the schools, diminishing any sense of dependency upon the state or 'the system' and heightening the need for entrepreneurialism. *Entrepreneurialism* is seen to follow as part of the new management culture of the 'school as enterprise', that is a releasing of the entrepreneurial skills of individuals within the organisation and the use of more 'effective' management models from the business world. (Goodchild & Holly, 1989; Keep, 1990). *Cost-effectiveness* in providing the service will be achieved by driving out the inefficiencies of 'the system', the bureaucratic inertia and the 'Town Hall politics' by devolving decisions to the schools. Finally, *'consumerism'* will privilege parents and employers in judging the quality of the education provided and reduce what is seen as the self-interested power of the producer lobby, i.e. the educationalists. The government wants to move towards an educational service that is differently provided and managed, in which high choice and diversity will create the basis for a new relationship within schools, between schools and around schools. In the 'natural environment' of the market, free from the 'contamination' of a system, schools should release the 'natural' gifts of individuals; enterprise, initiative and the instinct for survival. The 'successful' schools will be those that become self-determining enterprises, promoting innovative and cost-effective approaches to fulfilling consumer demand. Removing the constraints of the system will allow the schools to 'do what should come naturally' (Keat & Abercrombie; 1991). This can be summed up by Figure 4.1.

MARKET DRIVEN		STATE SYSTEM
High	VS	Low
'choice/diversity'		'choice/diversity'

MANAGING CHANGE

Self-determining	*Systemic dependency*
and	and
Entrepreneurial	*Complacency*
Cost-effective	*Bureaucratic*
and	and
'Consumerist'	*'Protectionist'*

PROVIDING A SERVICE

FIGURE 5.1 *Market-driven versus state system*

We move on to present a school, referred to here as Flightpath Comprehensive, in which there is a degree of willingness to move towards the new ERA, but where changing the institutional practices is proving a formidable challenge. We argue here that the move from state provision to 'individualist', market-driven enterprises may well produce changes within schools that for the government are both unanticipated and unwelcome.

Local Management in Action

Going it alone

Transforming the 'old' into the 'new' revolves around freeing schools from the 'dead hand' of the LEAs and allowing them to decide, for themselves, how to spend the 'housekeeping money'. Within Flightpath Comprehensive the early perception among many senior staff, and the headteacher in particular, was that LMS genuinely offered an opportunity for schools to 'do their own thing' and break free from the financial and administrative constraints of the past, to become *self-determining*. In general terms, the constraints from the LEA were less to do with matters of policy and more to do with perceived 'inefficiencies' in the system:

> But I do believe firmly that schools often would be better managers of themselves, if they had more direct managerial control over finance and staffing and all the rest of it, so there's a lot of LMS that I welcome. And that's related not to any disaffection with our local authority officers, and the services that they provide. I mean they're all my friends, if you know what I mean, it's just that the more tiers you put into any structure the more noise you get in the system. And the noise in the system is often sheer, just sheerly frustrating. When the jobs get done they get done well. It's getting them done which has been the difficulty. (Deputy head, Interview, 28th September 1989)

The head's experiences of what he saw to be management problems in the LEA, (he was seconded to the LEA during the academic year 1989/90 to work on LMS) were sometimes shared with the SMC (Senior Management Committee) and tended to confirm people's suspicion that the LEA was occasionally unsure in its sense of direction and sometimes inefficient in carrying out its tasks. 'Going it alone' was increasingly seen as an opportunity to provide education more efficiently and effectively.

The school's firm belief in its own capacity to manage change helped to produce an enthusiasm to get to grips with LMS. Not just to start spending the money more wisely than the LEA, which was taken to be almost axiomatic among the SMC, but also to start managing in a more entrepreneurial, cost-effective and consumerist way. Early LMS training encouraged this and, after one training session, the Head asked one of the deputies to comment to the SMC on his view of the day:

> One thing to say is that it is nowhere near as frightening as people have given us to believe, as long as we are logical and sensible. (Deputy, SMC, 21 September 1989)   ▼

This confidence partly reflects the history of a school in which good management has been considered an important feature of school life. The Head has paid great attention to 'honing' the management structure and defining the job specifications of the senior managers. These skills of school management were seen as transferrable to managing 'the enterprise'; the rational and logical application of higher managerial skills were taken to be a necessary and sufficient basis for tackling the problems of institutional change. However, what was unclear was the extent to which models from the private business sector were applicable in the school (Keep, 1990) and there were fears about some of these models:

> At the moment there are a lot of cowboys, yuppie personnel, who are talking in terms of performance indicators as if they rule the world, and I'd only liken it to people who believe that the free enterprise economy is infallible. It isn't, and performance indicators can do as much damage as they can do benefit, if they are not sensibly determined and operated. And the thing that worries me is the combination of financial theories overriding educational philosophies combined with cost-cutting enterprises, using a criteria of performance as a cutting edge. (Deputy head, Interview, 28th September 1989)

This unease has been alluded to elsewhere (Bowe & Ball, 1990) and it is becoming increasingly clear that applying the principles of LMS to the development of school managerial systems is by no means straightforward.

> The Head was keen on devolving the INSET budget to departments, seeing it as a logical development from LMS, and a 'liberating idea': '. . . it is a sort of LMS for the departments' (Head). However, such a view was not embraced by one of the senior teachers who was concerned that deciding who was entitled to INSET was not in the hands of the heads of department (HODs), and it was therefore unfair to make them pay out of their budget. The Head then suggested that calculations could be made to compensate for the departmental differences in control over their budgets. (Observation notes: SMC, 18th January 1990)

Here there is an important difference between devolved budgeting and the making of financial policy. Who is to be involved in institutional policy making, and how, cannot be 'read-off' from the 1988 Act and, in practice, accommodating to the demands of the Act *in toto* has tended to mean that decision making increasingly rests with a small group of staff (Bowe & Ball, 1990; Ball & Bowe, 1990), pulling schools away from the new management styles of 'post-fordism' and back towards technocratic, hierarchical managerial styles:

> I mean, you cannot expect the classroom teacher — as we have in this school, a relatively young, inexperienced staff — to understand the finances of the school. There is this polarisation where your classroom teacher will concentrate on obviously trying to achieve the national curriculum, where the management, whilst very much aware of the

national curriculum, and what staff are trying to do, has also to balance the books on LMS. And certainly, I would suggest that for the very senior managers in the school — the head, the first deputy, the bursar — their minds have been concentrated very much on LMS during the last few months. (Senior teacher, Interview, 23rd March 1990)

Whether the school will begin to evolve more democratic and participatory management remains to be seen. However, the impact of LMS on many non-senior teachers has been to enhance their sense of exclusion from their working situation. In this sense the notion of self-determination only applies to a rather small section of the school's teachers.

Furthermore, a tension between the push for decentralisation and devolution and the continued concern for technical-scientific rationality and control is clearly evident (Harvey, 1990). This is more than a symptom of a transitionary phase, a temporary feature in which authority is used to develop ultimate freedoms. 'Self-determining' schools remain nested within a social world in which aspects of the 'self' (in institutional and individual terms) are partly determined elsewhere. For example, in Flightpath there has been a growing awareness that a major part of the budget will not be determined by the school, as the head made clear at a meeting of the middle/junior management:

I'm sure all this is the same for a lot of other schools and shouldn't we just decide upon the needs and be prepared to overspend? (Head of third year)

But that's the unreal world and it's not negotiable and you might as well accept that . . . I can assure you that there'll be no expansion in Westway and I could take you through the detailed economics of the formula and the rest. We've got high idealism and we'd need higher resources than we've got. It's as straightforward as that. (Head)

He then gave an example,

If it means you have to change your methods then that's what you'll have to do. I mean, chalk and talk is cheaper than a sort of individualised carousel and we'll just have to make those choices. (Head: curriculum council meeting, 5th March 1990)

Here financial self-determination appears to translate into financial constraint. Thus financial arguments for educational change are set *against* the professional judgements of teachers. It is hard to see this as either an indicator of greater efficiency or as a mechanism for raising standards, *unless* one accepts a priori that the teachers' judgements are always unsound. If one adds to this the need to respond to the externally imposed demands of the national curriculum then it is difficult to see the majority of teachers feeling any sense of self-determination. The dilemma is apparent in this comment from one of the deputy heads:

> I'd love to think LMS would solve that, but I can't see it. Under LMS we have formula funding with laws laid down from the outside and the bottom line is that group sizes may have to go up to get the flexibility we need to deliver the curriculum experiences we want to deliver. (Senior deputy, SMC, 8th February 1990)

Consequently we need to recognise that the possibilities for autonomous self-management are powerfully circumscribed by aspects of the budget over which schools may have little or no control. For example, those parts of the budget made up by: (a) the level of LEA expenditure (increasingly determined by the politics of the community charge); (b) the allocation via the 'formula' to each school (which has its own particular politics); (c) the vagaries of the local, micro-education markets (the levels of finance in bordering LEAs and the inherited pupil numbers and state of the 'plant' in neighbouring schools), as well as the potential for parental and employer sponsorship (thus raising the question of whether the new conditions of schooling allow all schools an equal opportunity to succeed).

Further, it is precisely the uncertainties introduced by this lack of autonomy that produces a sense of continual information deficit. Ironically a situation the SMC finds itself trying to resolve through 'tighter' administration and the active management of change. Thus devolution of management need not equal a devolution of power. As Ainley (1990) has suggested, LMS is in part an attempt by the Government to privatise the problems of financing schools. Thus, while self-determination appears to provide schools with new freedoms, it also opens them up to blame for their 'failures' and leaves them with the dilemmas and contradictions inherent in government policy, a policy they had little opportunity to 'determine'.

Being entrepreneurial

One way in which the Government is suggesting schools increase their level of self-determination is by making themselves far less dependent upon the state for all their finances. The 'added extra' which might provide greater budget flexibility could be found through a more *entrepreneurial* approach. This notion of enterprise in LMS refers to both the school as an organisation and to the people that work within it (Keat & Abercrombie, 1991). The government hopes schools will show enterprise by taking risks and being innovative in a commercial sense by modelling themselves on commercial enterprises, franchised to deliver the national curriculum. They also hope this new culture and philosophy of the 'school as enterprise' will release the entrepreneurial skills of individuals within the organisation. Wrapped up in the government's appeal for greater self-determination is the image of the macho world of the self-made man (*sic*): the individual whose drive, flair and initiative seizes the present and builds the future. The new culture of enterprise in schools will produce better management (of money and people) and the generation of new sources of income.

Within Flightpath, making the connections between financial concerns and educational concerns has not been straightforward. The major device has been the school management plan, which has dominated the work of the SMC for much of the year. Throughout that time there were frequent pleas from the senior managers for more time to 'ensure that the basics were still being done'; that matters of discipline, dealing with 'cover' and supply and pastoral work should not be neglected while trying to put together a management plan for the school. Being 'entrepreneurial' requires *time* to project income, to pursue additional income and to decide how this will be spent by somehow bringing educational aims and financial calculations into line. Finding that time has caused considerable problems:

> . . . there is a tendency to say, look, this is where the buck stops, finance wise, if you haven't got the money you can't do it, but not to apply the same sort of stringency when you're talking about staff time and resources. We've only got a limited amount of staff time resources, we can't handle this, this is where it stops . . . bang (Senior deputy, Interview, 16th January 1990)

The outcome has been incredible pressure on senior staff to 'deliver' a new, entrepreneurial management thrust while trying to keep hold of the educational issues that 'won't go away'.

Furthermore, getting a clear picture of future income has been no easy matter:

> In purely financial terms we ought to know the missing links in a year's time, therefore we ought to have that final certainty, we ought to have that final clarity. I think what will then happen is that the certainty will maybe dictate to us, small though resources are, what we have relative to what we put into our management plan, and we might then say that we've in fact not prioritised. You see that's another thing, we've drawn up priorities in the SMC but against what? We don't know, and so it might well be that we've been hopelessly optimistic about our resources. (Senior deputy, Interview, 16th January 1990)

Innovation, risk and enterprise tend to flourish in a context where the risks can be calculated, income can be calculated and the consequences of failure are acceptable. In these respects the conditions at Flightpath are not particularly favourable. Despite this they have 'taken a risk' with a new sports hall, jointly funded by the LEA and a loan to the school. The long-term problem will be the servicing of the debt. Already the need to repay parts of the loan before the hall starts to earn significant amounts of money from outside is giving cause for concern: 'The burden of the sports hall means we really do need a generous local benefactor to see us through' (Head, SMC, 29th January 1990). More recently the Head (SMC, 14th May 1990) has observed, 'There's not the money available in industry that there was and it's now got to the point where the time spent chasing it may be too much.' It remains to be seen how much impact the funding of a debt will have upon the educational processes of the school in the next few years. But in taking on this new responsibility the school has become tangled up in the leisure and financial markets, both notoriously unstable in the last few years. Educational survival may now be open to the fluctuations of markets over which the school will have little control; potentially eroding further the sense of self-determination as the school tries to respond to a variety of very different markets. Thus, for Flightpath, self-determination and market-driven funding may come to stand in stark opposition to one another. It is indeed sobering to note that the 'Thatcherite' dream of economic revival based upon flourishing small businesses has actually produced a high number of failures and casualties in the small business sector of the economy.

At the individual level of enterprise Flightpath promoted a member of staff to the position of marketing manager, in September 1989, although he retains responsibility for IT in the school and is therefore limited in the time he has to pursue his marketing role. Nevertheless, in the SMC meetings at the end of 1989 questions of marketing and seeking funds externally became so frequent the following appears in the observation notes:

> Note: Conversation with senior deputy re the appearance of 'marketing' as a vital sub-text of the meeting. He feels the establishment of the marketing group and the appointment of a marketing manager has been important here. (Observation notes, SMC, 2nd October 1989)

Although 'raising peoples consciousness' of marketing has had an impact upon their way of seeing educational issues it does not mean the contradictions between educational and marketing issues are any easier to resolve. The major financial success of the marketing manager has been to secure a suite of computers by getting a computer firm to use the school's name in a national advertising campaign. While this will undoubtedly provide short-term flexibility elsewhere in the budget such sources of funding do tend to come in the form of 'one-off' deals. They cannot provide for long-term stability, predictability or continuity in the level of funding. Long-term planning may therefore become difficult and increasingly limited to the 'known' aspects of funding, thus in effect restraining the sought after flexibility.

Getting value for money

The other side of the planning coin relates to expenditure. The government intends LMS to encourage schools to be *cost effective*. Interestingly, effectiveness and efficiency as conceptions for planning are confused and welded together in such a notion. Deciding the cost of books, laboratory equipment or paper has never been a difficult task. Neither is it an insurmountable problem to locate or monitor overall staff costs or the cost of repair work on the school:

> These figures are illustrative of those that have been submitted to the DES. If we have to have a 4% cut in our budget, if we have to shed £70,000 and staff are 80% of our budget it's tempting to cut 4.5% of our staff. However, we could do it in other ways and therefore we do have to cost all the elements and that includes time. Time now costs money and we mustn't forget that. (Head, SMC, 30th October 1989)

The real difficulty lies in calculating the cost of 'activities', particularly teaching activities and then setting these against marketing or fund-raising. This is made even more problematic by the need to calculate the effectiveness of any activity. This is well illustrated in the next quote from observation notes:

> They talked about the use of spare capacity at Flightpath, i.e. the home economics room, the sports hall, etc. These are not in constant use and could be used by some of the primary schools from time to time:

> Perhaps we should pursue this and shouldn't charge them as a gesture of goodwill and as a good marketing strategy. (Senior teacher)

> Yes, I'd go along with that and we should look at it as a more cost-effective way of using our resources (Head, SMC, 8th February 1990)

Increasing the budget was set aside in order to market the school and its facilities and this was seen to be cost-effective. But there was no attempt in this instance to quantify the various elements and while the rhetoric was present the cost-benefit analysis was not. There has been frequent mention of the idea of an educational audit and some discussion of how the heads of department might be key figures in this process, but again finding time to do the calculations is not easy. Furthermore it is not certain that the skills necessary for such an audit are present within the school.

In a number of instances it appeared as if delegating the consequences of financial constraint assumed more importance than discussing the principles on which costs might be balanced with benefits.

There was then an exchange over the question of budget accountability and the matter of the cost of field courses was raised, in particular biology and geography.

It's very easy for people to say we'll do this course because someone else is picking up the bill. If we were to make it part of their departmental budget then they'd have to think about it, it would be helping people to become more aware of the cost of running their departments. (Head)

He then went on to suggest that music ought to have piano tuning as part of their budget.

Then they might choose to have only five pianos tuned each year instead of six. But it would be their choice. (Head)

One of the senior teachers was concerned that losing the field trips might seriously harm the marketing potential of the sixth form: 'I mean, if we're trying to attract kids back into the sixth form with interesting courses' (senior teacher). Controlling expenditure was brought back into the argument by another of the senior teachers and the Head raised the matter of administrative efficiency:

The advantage of keeping finance centralised is that I can negotiate the amount needed and not just allocate a fixed sum. People will always make sure they spend that fixed sum, even if they didn't need it. (Senior teacher)

Yes, and you can also save money on some of the costs and make sure that National Insurance and all the paperwork we need to ensure is done, gets done. (Head)

The educational concern of the first senior teacher was re-asserted.

By delegating you might end up with them being axed, in the long term. I'm a very firm believer in residential trips in educational terms. Have we thought about the possibility of some sort of sponsorship? (Senior teacher)

In this exchange cost-effectiveness is tangled up with educational concerns, consumerism and self-determination. Interestingly the issue remains unresolved and this may well reflect the contradictory nature of working with LMS, which presents schools with precisely the dilemmas that successive governments have failed to resolve. This is also apparent in the next quotations:

> The risk here is that if you devolve too much you generate more bureaucracy with all the different budgets. (Head)

> If you devolve everything too far then you don't become cost effective. (Senior teacher)

This opens up the whole question of centralisation versus devolution, *but* in a micro situation. We see here some of the same sort of solutions offered by members of the SMC as those suggested by politicians and social theorists for the state! 'Problems' for the management might be 'privatised' by getting other devolved budget holders to sort them out themselves (Ainley, 1990). (A cynical view might be that this is a way of passing on cost-cutting decisions to others. Self-determination is reduced to choices between alternative expenditures.)

Keeping the customers satisfied

Finally, in developing some criteria for cost-effectiveness the Act encourages schools to be aware of the consumers. There is evidence that in general terms the Head and a number of the senior management team embrace the notion of *consumerism*.

> What the client group want is very important and I applaud the prospective parents' questionnaire, but we really need to go further on this. (Head, SMC, 30th October 1989)

> The question of teaching the sixth form for a longer period at exam time was raised, because other schools were doing so and some parents had expressed concern. It was decided to look at this. (Observation notes, SMC, 8th February 1990)

But this is not a new phenomena at Flightpath.

> Well, those of us that have been in Flightpath school a long time, have been concerned about our image since 1968. When I came here in '68, the school was considered one of the worst schools in the Borough, both in terms of its pupil behaviour, its levels of attainment, its buildings. So since 1968 through various managers and through all the staff, including the help from parents, we have been constantly trying to improve the image of the school. Both from a visual point of view the introduction of

school uniform, which didn't exist in '68 in any form in the boys' school, through to raising the academic standards of the school. So we've been constantly working at that, and whilst one thinks that this is a new concept of marketing the school, it isn't. (Deputy head, Interview, 28th September 1989)

In the above quotation the consumers are defined in terms of the parents and the community. But students are also consumers and have to be attracted to the school and retained. The difficulty that emerges then is not just deciding who the customer actually is — parents, employers, students, or all of these — but which should have priority at any one time. In terms of entry to the school parents may be central, but then there is the question of retaining the commitment and involvement of the parents and the students, over time. Providing a 'student friendly' school with an enjoyable and well received curriculum, may not be the same as ensuring future parents will choose the school. Also what of employers who may find the traditional nature of the national curriculum unacceptable, how will they respond to requests for additional funding or for assistance on governing bodies? One 'solution' to this problem is offered in the Act which accords parents and employers greater privileges than the students, who are not statutorily required to be represented on the governing body, nor necessarily paramount in deciding which schools they go to. Far from being student-centred, the Act actually 'positions' students in the traditionally dependent learner role, the *real* consumers are parents and employers. This places key aspects of the teachers self-determination under threat:

> . . . for example, whilst this might be the ideal curriculum situation from their point of view, the realities are that we do have to provide an image to fulfil the requirement of the governors and the parents and I think one of the hardest areas that staff are trying to come to grips with at the moment is the reality that the governors and especially the parents, have a far greater say and influence in what goes on in the school, than they've ever experienced in the past. (Senior teacher, Interview, 23rd March 1990)

The SMC has been very aware of the extent to which 'image' and attracting the parents can present difficulties in meeting the individual needs of the students. Again we have the multiple account of the 'customer', do you meet community needs (the image parents want) or the needs of the individual students? Such questions are profoundly distorted by the introduction of differences in student worth.

> You are caught, and this is where LMS really raises its ugly head, in terms of true educational things. Each child has a price tag on it, and the sixth formers have the highest price tag, so in pure financial terms one

obviously is trying to raise the most amount of money you can. But Flightpath staff have always been conscious of our intake being skewed towards the less able child, and through the years we have developed what has got to be considered one of the best supportive education departments in the Borough. But of course the less able children tend not to stay on to the sixth form, unless we feel they are really going to benefit from it, and we have an excellent record, through our guidance department, of ensuring that our children get into employment as well. So you have this conflict of trying to ensure you've got a big sixth form, trying to ensure that you are really doing the best for the individual child, and the introduction of the disabled children. I don't think that's a sort of problem for us in terms of whether it was a bad image or not. I mean, I think personally it can do nothing but good for us but one has got to recognise the fact that these children do take a lot of extra time. (Senior teacher, Interview, 23rd March 1990)

Ironically, as Alder & Raab (1988) have pointed out, there is an interesting contradiction between increasing student numbers to gain greater income and the 'effectiveness' of the school. This may in turn have an impact on consumer demand. Consequently, if the DES insist upon the 1979 figures (though we have evidence that some LEAs are successfully circumventing these figures) the size of the school may actually count against the school, in the long term:

One of the most off-putting things that we've had to overcome in this school, is the size of the school: when I came here, we were a 12-form entry, over 2,000 children, over 120-odd teaching staff, and parents coming from small primary schools — and if they were the quieter, meeker children, were very intimidated. So we've had to work very hard at proving to them that big did not necessarily mean ugly and uncontrollable. (Senior teacher, Interview, 23rd March 1990)

Summary

The new educational world of self-determining schools, disciplined by the market, is intended to produce a social order in which the 'natural' talents and inclinations of individuals and organisations can come to the fore. However, our research suggests that far from releasing people from the burdens of bureaucracy LMS may well increase the internal administrative load. In addition 'being enterprising' requires risk capital and time. In the case study reported here, the former has been raised partly out of the 'system', but also via a loan at the unknown cost of linking the school's finance to the presently depressed leisure and financial markets. Responding to the consumers brings difficulties in tying together the competing concerns of parents, employers and students.

The picture is not one of new freedoms. Rather, the new elements introduced by LMS require schools to deal with a different, expanded and contradictory set of demands. In trying to adjust to these demands schools are finding the new era, constructed by others on the basis of neo-liberal and management theories, massively pressured and often a distraction from the world of educating students. Important issues about the purposes of schooling in our society are being thrown up by the implementation of LMS, but they are not being addressed in public debate. The assumption of the superiority of the market appears unassailable. But perhaps we can leave the last word to the senior deputy at Flightpath:

> If you just take the sports hall. You've had two out of four deputy heads intimately involved in setting it up, one from the resourcing point of view, one from the business management point of view. We had one senior teacher who is also very much involved in the nuts and bolts of it. You've got those three working all hours, those three really working early in the morning for the last six months. It's a huge soaking up of energy and somebody somewhere along the line has to evaluate that and say, 'Is that part of the global target of the school?' (Senior deputy, Interview, 28th November 1990)

Note

1. This paper is a considerably shortened version of the BERA 1990 paper 'The Spirit is willing but the flesh is weak: An exploration of LMS in one secondary school'.

6 'It's a Long Way from Teaching Susan to Read': Some Preliminary Observations from a Project Studying the Introduction of Local Management of Schools

JANE BROADBENT, RICHARD LAUGHLIN, DAVID SHEARN and NIGEL DANDY

Introduction

The introduction of local management of schools (LMS) is part of a wave of such initiatives in the public sector. The philosophy behind these initiatives is reflected in the financial management initiative (FMI), outlined in the White Paper (1982) 'Efficiency and Effectiveness in the Civil Service'. The aim of the ideas in the White Paper was to change the role of the public servant from that of administrator to that of manager. A feature of this change was the idea that organisations should become more responsive to their 'customers' and that the management of the financial resources should feature much more than previously. By making those who were responsible for spending the resources accountable for that expenditure it was hoped that resources would be used more effectively. This was partly premised on the idea that those closer to the situation knew best what was needed and could make decisions faster, but also on the notion that those who made decisions should be responsible for the financial implications of their decisions.

The White Paper can also be seen as a vehicle for introducing the notion of 'management' rather than 'administration' into the public sector. In the sense in which these terms are used here, administration requires a role oriented to stewardship of given resources and to the implementation of decisions taken elsewhere. Management offers much more chance to develop decisions and polices, and, perhaps in the longer term, even to generate resources.

In this paper we will consider the extent to which these changes are affecting the culture of the school — an organisation geared traditionally to teaching, with little responsibility for management. In order to do this we will first consider the changes which are being implemented following the 1988 Education Reform Act (ERA) arguing that LMS is imbued with a very different philosophy of 'what a school is about' than that which previously existed in the schools. Some findings from fieldwork with four schools will be introduced to illustrate the way in which teachers, clerical staff, and governors, are handling their new roles and responsibilities. Finally an analysis using some models of change (Laughlin, forthcoming) will be made and some tentative conclusions about the extent of the change will be offered.

The Legislation and the Context in which it is Implemented

The basic principles of the FMI include a statement about the nature of 'good management'. This involves having a clear view of objectives, along with means to assess and, where possible, measure outputs or performance in relation to these objectives. Along with this goes the responsibility for making best use of resources, including scrutiny of outputs and value for money. Finally, information, training and access to expert advice should be available to ensure that responsibilities can be carried out. Cost information is mentioned particularly. Richards (1987) points out that behind this is the implicit assumption that management is control, and that control is about budgeting. Hence accounting issues are important to FMI. Also, in seeking to define responsibilities closely, there has been a move toward delegation to lower-level managers. In some cases this delegation is giving new and very different responsibilities to those who in the past have been much more closely concerned with the administration of a service, and whose main concern therefore has been with service provision. Thus, for many FMI has led to a fundamental change in the nature of their jobs, and this change provides them with a central role in the budgetary control process.

The practical implications are that FMI has delegated authority down to 'managers' rather than administrators, and that 'good managers' exercise a strongly budgetary role. This kind of philosophy is also apparent in the notion of LMS.

LMS has moved the management of schools down to the level of the school although certain key issues, such as the amount of resources globally available to the education service and to specific schools, remain with the local authority. While the global budget allocated to education in total can be decided by the local authority, the amounts delegated to each school must be allocated using a formula. The idea behind this is to try to provide schools with some means of forecasting their budgets and thereby allow forward planning. This delegation has made schools financially accountable. ERA has also made them accountable educationally via the national curriculum and assessment programmes. School governors are now, or will soon become, responsible for the allocation of the resources delegated by the formula. Given the definition of management inherent in LMS, and its close relationship to budgeting (as pointed out by Richards, 1987), then it is not surprising that the management delegated to the schools involves financial aspects and particularly financial planning and control — budgeting.

Whatever the detail of each Local Education Authority's (LEA) formula, more than 75% of money going to schools is allocated on an age-weighted basis. There is, then, an accountability structure built into the relationship between the school and the community which is given visibility in financial terms. Each pupil entering a school brings with them a tranche of funds. It is argued that the schools must be responsive to the needs of 'their clients'. An unresponsive school will lose pupils and the funds it needs to survive.

To be educationally viable each school requires enough resources to be able to offer a wide enough curriculum to provide a balanced programme, as defined by the national curriculum. It must be financially viable in that it must be able to pay sufficient teachers and must have sufficient physical resources (buildings, equipment, heating and books, for example) to provide that curriculum. Given the fact that some expenses are fixed regardless of the number of pupils in the school, and that educational concerns may provide parameters for such things as class size, the balancing of financial and educational matters becomes very complex. The rationale behind all this is that 'consumer' choice will ensure that 'good' schools survive as they will attract pupils and funding. 'Bad' schools which do not attract pupils and funding will, given the same logic, fail. Accountability to the 'consumer' is therefore embedded in a financial relationship, and financial viability is used as a proxy for educational viability.

Accountability rests formally with the governing body in delegated schools, but it is the headteacher who carries this responsibility on a day-to-day basis. Thus at school level new tasks are being introduced as the intertwining of the educational and financial is introduced. Previously some financial recording has been done, but on a very minor level in comparision to the new requirement. It is the intrusion of the financial elements in a very explicit fashion, at the level of the school, which provides the most radical element of the LMS initiative. The effects of the imposition of financial issues into the school forms the focus of our study. We are researching the way in which these new procedures and responsibilities impact on the environment of the school. As the headteacher of one of the schools with which the team are working commented early in the study, 'It's a long way from teaching Susan to read'.

In the next section we will go on to examine some of the experiences of the four schools with which the team are working.

The Schools

In our research we are undertaking a longitudinal study of four schools in one LEA. The schools are different in many ways; two are primary, two are secondary, small and large schools are represented in both the primary and secondary sectors, as are different socio-economic areas. Two are 'losers' and two are 'winners' in the reallocation of resources which have resulted from the implementation of formula funding, although these may be dubious titles given overall budget reductions in the LEA. It should be recognised that although the four schools represent some diversity they are not a representative sample.

Picton

Picton is a large comprehensive school with approximately 1,200 pupils aged from 12 to 18. It lies within a middle-class area of a large northern city. It has approximately 70 staff, including a headteacher and three deputy heads. Its clerical and administrative support comprises a registrar, an assistant registrar, three clerical/secretarial assistants and a recent and temporary appointment of a full-time clerical assistant to deal specifically with financial aspects of LMS. The capitation in 1989/90 was of the order of £40,000; the devolved budget for 1990/91 is just over £1.8 million. The school is one of the winners, but because of a declining budget overall the amount allocated barely covers current levels of activity.

The introduction of the devolved budgets and the related financial matters have been largely absorbed by a very small group of teachers, clerical staff and governors. The involvement of the other teaching staff and many governors has been minimal. The small group who are involved with LMS are, in large measure, now doing very different jobs from previously, and from the majority of their colleagues. Three themes help to illustrate this.

First is the nature of the group and the extent to which its members are comfortable in dealing with the new tasks. The small group who are carrying the financial issues are known as the 'LMS Group'. It comprises the headteacher, one of the deputies, and to some extent the chair of governors. Working with them is the registrar and the new clerical assistant taken on to deal specifically with these issues. A senior teacher, moved sideways from a head of department role, now has major responsibilities for buildings and land, but is less centrally involved than the others. This group has absorbed all the workload which LMS has involved. The strain and stress on the members of this group has been enormous.

Because of the introduction of competitive tendering within areas of service formerly provided exclusively by the local authority (such as works, recreation and cleansing), delegated schools have inherited contracts previously negotiated with these organisations. Headteachers of schools with delegated budgets have not been happy simply to accept the prices and levels of service represented in the contracts they have inherited, and have therefore re-negotiated terms with the service departments. They have also organised pressure groups to review the delivery of these services, and the processes for rendering bills from the service department to the schools and approving charges at school level. Members of the LMS Group at Picton have been involved in all these activities. These new activities are inevitably outside the remit that teachers might have expected when they entered the profession and their lack of experience in such matters has generated much stress.

This stress has been greatest on the teacher members, as they have experienced great role conflict in adopting the new managerial role. At Picton the head has described himself as speaking a 'different language' from the rest of the staff, and claims that more of his time is spent talking to cleaners, caretakers and contractors than to the teaching staff. The other two members of teaching staff involved in the team are in a similar situation; they are effectively isolated from their colleagues who have no experience of LMS, and currently no interest in such issues. An example of this lack of interest is given by an informal comment of a teacher-governor (who might be expected to have a more direct interest than some of the other teachers) at one governors meeting, 'What is this to do with me?' when confronted with a set of financial papers.

This reluctance to become involved in LMS issues is not only held by the teaching staff; even the registrar, who previously had some responsibilities for the capitation monies of the school, is not very happy about the responsibilities thrust on her by its introduction.

The second issue is the extent to which attempts have been made to involve more people in these issues. The newly formed finance subcommittee of the governors met for the first time in February 1989 to consider the draft formula-funding arrangements produced by the LEA. The responses it produced were largely the work of the LMS Group. The Group did not meet again until June 1989 when the capitation allowance for the year and its allocation to departments was decided. Again it relied on the existing machinery within the school (the school finance committee) to deal with the detail. Following the appointment of a new chair of governors, it met again in November 1989, now with a new set of members. This meeting along with another in January 1990 began the task, but not until March 1990 did it agree a 'standstill budget', already prepared by a sub-set of the LMS Group. Since June 1990 monthly meetings throughout the school year have been planned and held. The group are anxious to try to find some more 'management types', to try to expand the team which are managing the increasingly complex contractual and budget problems, but this is difficult even at the governor level. Recent co-options have been geared to this need.

The third issue is the lack of impact of LMS on the school more generally. The school set up a working group, one of a number of such working and curricular groups planned to feed ideas into a steering committee, which, in turn, would feed policy recommendations to the senior management team. It was intended to be a development of the finance committee which made recommendations about capitation. It met twice, amid confusion about its role, and concentrated on trying to 'educate' its members about the nature of LMS. Attempts were also made to involve the general staff in such an 'educational' exercise. Two sessions were held but, in both, staff again were unsure of why this was taking place and were highly suspicious. From December 1989 no further attempts have been made to involve the mainstream teaching staff in LMS, although there is currently a review of internal committee structures. Changes resulting from this may, in the future, lead to greater intrusion of financial considerations into school activities. To date, however, LMS is peripheral to the major activities and concerns of the teachers and the school members more generally.

Topgate

Topgate also lies in the middle-class area of the city. It is a middle school of approximately 380 pupils in the age group of 8–12 years old. It opened in the autumn of 1974 in new purpose-built premises. The present headteacher was appointed in 1976. In addition to the head are 14 full-time-equivalent teaching staff, a deputy head, a general assistant and a school secretary. The current chair of governors is a parent of a pupil, although an LEA appointee. The previous chair of governors, who resigned in July 1990, was a parent governor. Most of the governors are parents of pupils, or ex-pupils, of the school or have other direct links with it, being teacher or staff representatives. The governing body as a whole is very supportive of the headteacher and the school. The budget of this school is of the order of £412,000 this financial year (1990/91), a huge increase over the previous amount which had to be controlled at school level, the capitation allowance of around £9,000. This school has benefited from the introduction of the formula method of funding, and has been able to introduce modest increases in its staffing levels, amounting to 0.3 of a teacher's time. This has freed the deputy to 'become a proper deputy' (in the words of the headteacher) and allows her to shed a half-time classteacher responsibility, leaving her free to teach across the school and 'know all the children in the school' (in her own words).

Although the school is very different from Picton, the financial aspects of LMS are similarly restricted to a small group of people. The headteacher is very clear that this is his policy, commenting to his staff on one occasion (when they were invited to attend a course about LMS), 'There's no real need for you to go, I keep you informed of what you need to know at staff meetings. In these times when there is so much that is new, division of labour is a good thing, and its better that you stick to the curricular matters.' At the end of the academic year, when discussing overall progress of the LMS initiative he commented, 'I act as a buffer, a filter to protect the rest of the staff from the huge amount of issues, many of which are not important and would only upset them if they had to contend with them.'

Hence financial issues in the school are largely dealt with by the head. There is some involvement of the deputy, and the secretary is involved in the recording aspects. The governing body has formed a subcommittee to deal with financial affairs. This comprises the head, his deputy, the chair of governors and four other governors. Attendance at the meetings is very good considering that they are held at 4 p.m. on a working day (on average only one person will be missing), and the governors are all working people. So far the main governing body has not been closely involved in the financial decision making, and has ratified decisions made by this subcommittee with little comment.

The financial decisions which have been made so far are ones which have involved spending extra resources. The key figure in the process is the headteacher. He takes advice from his staff via staff meetings and has been known to alter his decisions in line with their advice. However, he is the main instigator of ideas and, in discussions, the staff have often commented that they do not know enough to make final decisions. They are happy to leave things with the head, provided he has considered relevant issues which they have raised.

Formally the financial decisions are made in the finance committee, and here the head brings issues, usually after airing them with the staff. The reaction of the governors is similar to that of the staff. Questions are usually raised to probe the boundaries of familiar issues, for example one governor is involved in sales of office equipment, and raised questions about the form of a potential lease agreement for the supply of computer equipment. However, much is left to the discretion of the head, particulary as regards issues of principal, as governors argue that he is the one with greatest knowledge about such things. This is frequently tempered by a query as to what the staff as a whole think about the issues. Thus, even in the arena of the finance committee, the involvement of the members is somewhat limited and the headteacher's views carry great weight.

The headteacher has made no attempt to extend the involvement of the staff in financial affairs. The finance committee has been extended to include a member who is closely involved in local politics. The benefit which accrues from this is not technical, but it does provide more information about the overall policies and financial situation of the local authority.

Internal school structures have not been changed to deal with LMS; the existing system of year group meetings and a weekly staff meeting appears to be sufficient to deal with any financial matters. At governing body level a very sophisticated subcommittee structure (5 subcommittees, and an overall programme which has at least one meeting of either the whole body or one of the subcommittees every week of the school year) has developed to deal with school management. This has kept the finance function isolated, as the committee is delegated to make decisions as necessary. Such isolation may be breached in the near future as the LEA's financing arrangements for the next financial year involve changing the formula, and this may mean that the school is not as well off as it expected to be. The implications of this are so severe that the finance committee have felt obliged to call in the whole governing body to debate the issues. It remains to be seen to what extent this 'threat' changes the levels of involvement.

In summary, the experience at Topgate is very similar to that at Picton: LMS has been contained and few people have been involved with financial issues. This school appears to have always been organised very systematically and has managed the introduction of financial issues in a professional way. Systems have been extended rather than developed from scratch. Generally members of staff and governors have felt little need to become too concerned in the financial issues, perhaps because its systems were so well developed, and as yet no difficult financial decisions have had to be made.

This is not the case in the 'losing' schools were difficult financial decisions have had to be taken.

Fieldhouse

Fieldhouse School, a comprehensive school for children in the age range 11–16 years old, lies at the east of the city, isolated by a motorway which runs through the centre of its catchment area. Access problems have been created, and pupils who might live only a mile from the school, on a direct line, have to travel much further to negotiate the motorway. Even though there are school buses, many parents in the catchment area have chosen to send their children to more convenient schools elsewhere in the LEA. There is also some competition from a school in a neighbouring LEA only one and a half miles down the road. Thus, whilst the school population is now stable, the school which once had a population of 800 pupils now has only 300. There is a proposal from the Boundary Commissioners that the area cut off from the main city by the motorway should move to the neighbouring authority. This causes further uncertainty in the school, as its members feel that the outcome of such a move would be its closure. Thus the school can be seen to be fighting for its survival.

The area in which the school lies is one characterised by great social deprivation. About 55% of the pupils are from ethnic minority groups, mainly from the Indian subcontinent. Before LMS the school had a staff of 30 teachers for its 300 pupils, and it received special support for language teaching in the form of six teachers funded by Section 11 monies. Not infrequently the school will receive new pupils who have no English language at all. Also the pupils may be taken, by their parents, on extended visits of up to 12 months to visit relations abroad. Attendance overall is poor and parents may, for example, take children out of school on expeditions to buy clothes.

Whilst the results achieved by pupils of the school in public examinations are below average, it is nevertheless the view of staff that, given their intake, these results are good. There is some pride in the fact that there are only two children with Statements of Special Educational Need. These were ones who brought their Statements from their primary school, and the school policy is to avoid this procedure which is seen as providing a stigma for the child.

The links with the local community are strong. The headteacher works hard at these, regularly attending Mosque committee meetings. Local members of the community are represented on the governing body, but do not contribute significantly. Parental support is not very forthcoming. The last Parents' Meeting was linked to a social event, intended to fulfil the needs of all, including the ethnic community. No parent attended.

The long-term survival of the school is much less certain than for any of the others we are studying. The reasons include boundary and demographic changes but the introduction of LMS has had a further impact. There is now much less money available, the school has lost much of the special protection that the LEA previously provided. Hence the school needed to shed three teachers to make the books balance.

This was done by a process of 'natural wastage' and voluntary redeployment. As one of those leaving was a deputy head, the headteacher suggested that the organisation of the school be adjusted to incorporate only one deputy rather than two. This tactic produced savings at the management level, giving some protection to the teaching staff. Even so, criticism came from teaching staff at the head's decision to move one of them to teach a subject in which he had trained but had not subsequently taught. This ensured that no compulsory redeployment was necessary. Similarly a post dealing with careers was also lost as the head argued that 'all staff can deal with careers'. Again this promoted discussion and dissent, but provided some protection of the mainstream teaching of subject areas.

As the head aimed to protect the mainstream teaching of the school as well as the jobs of the staff who wished to remain at the school, the status quo was maintained as much as possible. This was perceived to provide the best educational experience for pupils. Hence resourcing problems did not force any reappraisal of the mode of educational provision. It simply led to the abandonment of some less central activities and a marginal reorganisation of some teaching loads.

Despite the very serious financial situation, the team dealing with LMS issues is, as in the other schools, very small. Formally the group is named the Finance and Personnel Committee, and comprises members of the governing body, representatives of staff, the LEA and parents. The headteacher is centrally involved and has worked with the chair of governors to steer through some reorganisation of the staff, which has allowed the redeployment of existing staff to posts vacated by resignations. It is the power of the head working in consort with the chair of governors which we have observed in the meetings we attended.

Despite the fact that the financial situation is a cause for concern throughout the school, there is little evidence of significant attempts to involve the staff as a whole in the issues of LMS. The teacher-governors do seem to have presented the views of 'the staff' — this of course is their function — but there is little evidence of involving the wider staff on a practical level, and their concern centres around the curricular and staffing issues. The staff would like to see a split of the finance and personnel committee into two different committees in order that finance should not be seen to be the determining factor all the time.

At the governing body level there is little involvement of the wider membership, and some evidence that those closely involved are less than enthusiastic about their position. The current chair of governors has, after nine months of LMS, announced that he will be resigning his post.

Overall the position at Fieldhouse is rather chaotic. However, the pressures on the school have been exacerbated, but not totally created by the LMS initiative. The coping mechanisms have been very similar to those in the other schools. Only a few members of the community have been involved and little attempt has been made to extend the circle. There is clear evidence that the 'classroom teachers' in this school shun the impingement of the financial issues on the curricular and educational issues. The structures which have developed have produced a subcommittee of the governing body to deal with the financial issues, and no attempt has been made to develop the issues further.

Queen Mary

Queen Mary is a nursery first school of approximately 153 first school pupils, and 80 part-time nursery attenders. The school has also lost resources. It lies within a poor urban area, at the edge of a large council estate, at the junction of several busy roads. There are no green fields around, and the playground is mainly tarmac, although efforts have been made to put down special surfaces and provide play equipment to make the environment more interesting. The site is shared with the middle school and several local authority offices which are not directly concerned with education. This creates problems for the headteacher in controlling expenditure, as the 'services' to the site are shared and the costs apportioned to the different units on site may not reflect their own usage. This means that there are fewer elements over which the headteacher has direct control.

The resources which the headteacher now controls are of the order £245,000, a huge increase on the £4,000 which used to be available as the capitation allowance. Quantitative increases of this nature have qualitatively altered the nature of the financial control function at school level. The headteacher anticipated that the changes in overall funding created by the formula would mean that the school would have a shortfall in resources compared with the previous situation. Thus he arranged that when one of the caretakers retired (before the delegation) a part-time post rather than a full-time one was created. Also a child care assistant was given help to gain early retirement. Despite these efforts one teacher and two 'dinner-ladies' were declared surplus to requirement.

This decision to declare job-losses was steered through the governors meeting by the headteacher and the chair of governors. As 80% of expenditure is on salaries, savings on staffing were inevitable. In arriving at this decision the headteacher worked through all elements of expenditure: power, cleaning costs, and consumables such as paper and pencils. Having calculated the bare minimum needed for these he then examined the staffing which could be afforded and the way in which teaching could be organised with this number of staff. This was then examined to see if it was educationally viable and the decision was made that it was.

The school has managed the complex processes efficiently, in that staff have perceived the cuts as being applied 'fairly'. Three classrooms have been joined together, to create a more open-plan space. The end result is seen by the staff as a better educational atmosphere, despite the loss of the teacher. Thus the situation which has arisen from the financial stringency has been justified in educational rather than economic terms. The headteacher is of the opinion that any further reductions in the resources available would make it difficult to provide an educational experience of the same quality for the children.

Despite the size and gravity of the resourcing problem, those involved in LMS are few in number. The main 'players' in the LMS team are the head and the chair of governors. The deputy head is involved peripherally, as is the one member of staff who is on the governing body, and the school secretary is closely involved in the record keeping.

Structures in the school have changed very little following the introduction of LMS. The governing body has not sub-divided to form a finance committee and no extra committees have been formed at school level. There has been an increase in the number of governors meetings, from one a term to one a month (in term time), in order to try to involve the whole governing body in the new responsibilities attached to the delegation to school level. This was a result of a positive decision taken by the head and the chair of governors, who decided that there were insufficient people on the governing body to make a subcommittee structure sensible. The school has had difficulties in finding parent governors and co-opted governors from the local community. Many of the current governors are connected with the school, not only because they have children there, but also because they work there in some capacity, such as caretaker or dinner-lady. Having young children makes it difficult for many to get to meetings, and training sessions for governors held across the city in tertiary colleges are difficult for them to attend.

The tactic of involving the governing body as a whole might be seen as an attempt to try to extend the size of the LMS group. To some extent it has been successful, as a core of the governing body has attended regularly. However some members have dropped out completely and, of those attending, some have not contributed much to the decision-making process. Thus the decisions are made mainly by the headteacher and the chair of governors. These decisions are discussed by the governing body, and can be modified there, but this meeting is not the main source of decisions.

In summary, the effects of the introduction of LMS has been remarkably similar in all the schools. While the schools have had to cope with different problems, they have all kept LMS within a small group of people both at school and governor level. They have developed systems to record the requisite data; they have entered into the decision-making process. Thus the steering media of the organisations have changed. The delivery of education has also changed slightly in three out of the four schools — those which have had staffing changes as a result of the new resourcing situation. In all cases the changes have been justified by educational arguments.

It appears that the educational values of the school remain intact. Nowhere has there been heard an argument that any of the schools' activities should be stopped or reduced because of the economic or financial reasons only. The economic issues generated by LMS remain peripheral, located with small groups of people. There has been little impingement on the activities of classroom teachers.

Towards an Analysis

The field-work is underpinned by a particular theoretical and method-ological approach. The theory is seen as a skeleton which can be only understood fully by its being 'fleshed out' by the empirical details of a particular situation. As such the theory will inform and be informed by the field-work. The approach to the field-work is discourse-based and centrally concerned with communication. It relies on the engagement of both those who are researching, and those who are the subject of the research. The approach, which will be discussed in more detail next, is therefore an example of what has been called 'middle range thinking' (Laughlin, 1990). A central issue in all this work (which may be referred to in detail in Laughlin, 1987, 1991; Broadbent, Laughlin & Read, 1991; Power & Laughlin, 1990; Broadbent, 1991) is the idea of the 'lifeworld', the values and beliefs which are formed discursively over time and which are argued to be held by groups of people, either on a societal or organisational level.

A second issue is that of organisational change. Laughlin (1991), develops four different models of change. Two describe change of a 'first order', which does not involve a change in the lifeworld of the organisation in question. Two describe 'second order change', where the organisational lifeworld is changed. The change in the schools is argued to be of a first order; this is because the central values of the school which relate to 'education' have not been changed by the introduction of financial issues at school level.

There are, however, two models of first order change. The first model of first order change is called *rebuttal*. Here the intended change is rebutted and the disturbance caused is short term. Rather 'stronger' is the second model of change, *reorientation*, where systems do become changed, but in such a way that the values in the lifeworld are not compromised. Our case is that this is the type of change which is occurring in the four schools.

This type of change is argued to be the result of the tendency for only small groups of people to become involved in LMS, so as to 'protect' the mainstream activities of the school. On the face of it this might appear to be a useful course of action. Classroom teachers certainly have a sufficient burden of dealing with curricular matters. Their reluctance to become involved perhaps indicates their willing acceptance for LMS to fall on others. It is a strategy which leaves them able to do what they 'came into teaching to do'.

However there remains the possibility that the lifeworlds of those involved in LMS might change. Given that the lifeworld is developed through discourse, those who are involved in LMS may well develop a lifeworld which takes on board the values of LMS. Thus second order change may develop in the members of the LMS group and the lifeworld of the school as a whole may become fragmented (see Broadbent (1991) for a fuller account of this type of situation). This may not happen. The values in the educational system may be secure enough to ensure that the change process remains at the 're-orientation' stage. Different situations may develop in different schools. This detail can only be found in the context of particular empirical situations. Some organisations may keep their educational values throughout the school, while others may become 'schizoid' (Laughlin, 1991), having different lifeworlds within different groups of organisational members. This may then lead to conflict within the organisation. Thus a tactic taken in good faith to protect the values of the school must be reorganised to have potential drawbacks. Indeed three out of the four heads have spoken to the researchers, at different times, of 'speaking a different language'.

The process of change will continue, and it is the aim of the research group to follow the process in detail at the schools with which we are involved. In continuing the detailed case work, the question of evaluation remains to be asked. Has the delegation of financial management to school level done anything to improve the education of our children? So far it is clear that the implementation of LMS has been such as to 'protect the school' and maintain the status quo and the decisions that are taken have always been 'sanitised' by relating them back to educational values. The 'cost' of this absorption has been high, locking key senior staff (particulary the headteachers) into routine clerical and administrative tasks. Can this be good for 'teaching Susan to read'? Such an evaluation cannot be made at this stage since the changes are still working through the schools. Our work continues with the aim to see what the future holds in the schools in question.

7 Finding Simple Answers to Complex Questions: Funding Special Needs under LMS

TIM LEE

Introduction

The theme of this chapter is that local management of schools (LMS) policy forces Local Education Authorities (LEAs) to adopt crude solutions to extremely complex problems in the allocation of resources for special needs. The term special needs is used to refer to pupils with learning difficulties and also to needs arising due to social disadvantage. The approach is critical. The aim is to highlight areas where LMS policy may have or does have negative consequences for special needs provision. The organisation of the chapter is as follows. First there is a discussion of 'maximum delegation' to schools — the cornerstone of LMS. The implications of reducing LEA central services and the future of centrally funded special educational provision are considered. The second section reviews formula funding, exposing five issues of concern. In the third section on school management the potential effect of LMS on the allocation of resources within schools is considered. The conclusion argues that while past methods of funding special needs were not ideal, LMS in many ways restrains authorities from equitably funding schools according to their needs.

Maximum Delegation

LMS is designed 'to secure the maximum delegation of financial and managerial responsibilities to governing bodies' (DES, 1988a: para. 10). The government has therefore imposed restrictions on the amounts LEAs can hold back from schools. The intention is that in the future only 'a limited number of services will continue to be provided centrally by the LEA' (DES, 1988a: para.

68

10). These developments are likely to have a significant impact on LEA-provided services for children with special needs.

Services provided free by the LEA have traditionally been an important source of support for schools and pupils. In the early years of LMS this tradition lives on, the majority of LEAs choosing to retain direct control over the allocation of school psychological and educational welfare services, home tuition, peripatetic and advisory teachers, provisions for statemented pupils and funding for special units in mainstream schools. (Special schools are funded from a separate budget.)

Over the next few years, however, the evolution of LMS will demand that the educational customs of many areas are broken. LEA services face a period of instability and change. The government is placing increasingly restrictive limits on LEA central spending, the latest emerging in DES regulations issued in December 1990. From 1993, all authorities must delegate at least 85% of the amount theoretically available to schools — the potential schools budget (PSB) (DES, 1990b). This provides a fairer system of capping LEAs than that operating in the period 1990–93 — limiting discretionary exceptions has proved itself an arbitrary method. However the new delegation target is extremely demanding. Not only does it require that LEAs change their plans in mid course, directing their attention towards a new set of government targets, but DES figures show that in 1990/91 only 11 authorities delegated more than 80% of their PSB and none reached 85% (DES, 1990a). This data, often referred to as the 'Section 42 league table' can also be used to estimate the scale of delegation which is being called for. Collectively, LEAs in England must cut in the order of £850 million from their central budgets by April 1993.

In this hostile climate for all central services, the options for LEAs are limited. Cuts can be made or resources can be delegated. Services dealing with children's special needs are in many ways better placed than others to resist unwelcome change. Finance for the statutory duties of LEAs, such as the assessment of pupils under the 1981 Act, cannot be passed to schools. Other services which are non-statutory but for which the client is primarily the pupil and not the school, as in the work of education welfare officers, may also be retained by LEAs if they can prove 'that the needs of pupils can only be targeted effectively if provision is retained centrally' (DES, 1988a: para. 80). Funding for teams of peripatetic and advisory teachers can be held centrally if LEAs can demonstrate to the DES that central control is the only way to guarantee that (a) pupils continue to receive specialist tuition, or that (b) this is the only means of ensuring central teams of 'reasonable size' (DES, 1988a: para. 81). The jobs of peripatetic SEN teachers certainly appear safer than those of peripatetic music teachers in most areas.

In general, most LEAs will delegate the costs of central support for special needs only as a last resort. However, some authorities are keen to dissuade schools from opting out of LEA control for purely financial reasons — schools receive a 'cash bonus' in lieu of their share of the central services budget if they become grant maintained.

Cambridgeshire LEA (1990) has issued plans to notionally devolve the total of the PSB to schools. However this is not '100 percent' delegation as such because schools will be required to pay back to the LEA sums to pay for the LEA's statutory services and for other key central services agreed to 'add value' to education in schools. The delegation of resources for special educational needs provision is described as an area 'where particular care and caution will be necessary'. However the main obstacle to devolving resources for pupil support for special needs is not because the LEA will lose control over the provision but because the formula for delegating resources is seen as insufficiently fair in its operation.

Whether by choice or compulsion, central services in most areas face reorganisation. The DES has sketched out the type of 'agency' approach which LEAs might follow (DES, 1990b: paras. 37–8, 61–2). Wherever possible LEA services should be financed at least partly, perhaps wholly, by fees charged to schools. They will be forced to compete for custom because schools (a) will not be obliged to purchase services, and (b) if they do decide that agency support is needed they will be able to buy services from their own LEA, neighbouring authorities and other suppliers which might emerge. As a result, many of the government's aims for LMS will be promoted. These aims are: reducing the central spending of LEAs; making the costs of services visible to schools; empowering heads and governors; subjecting LEA services to market forces; and breaking the monopoly of LEAs as service providers. Competition is the key. The theory is that LEA services will be forced to learn the 'three E's' of the new age in education — economy, efficiency and effectiveness. They will also be forced to respond more closely to the demands of their clients because their size or even survival rests on their competitiveness and the willingness of schools to buy their services.

The reality of the agency approach may be different to the theory. There are fears that schools are not always best placed to make decisions over the use of services. Specialists may be under-utilised, leading to cuts in services and job losses. When given the choice to buy in support and advice, local managers are not obliged to. Outside support may be seen as unnecessary or, most worryingly, unaffordable. There will be great incentives to 'make do and mend'. This was predicted by the Coopers & Lybrand (1988) report at the inception of LMS:

> If schools had the responsibility to 'buy in' psychological, welfare or medical services, such resource decisions would need to be balanced against their other demands for scarce resources. This might encourage a tendency in schools to under-purchase such services and seek to make do with staff less professionally qualified, perhaps at the expense of the pupil(s) concerned. (Coopers & Lybrand, 1988: para. 2.65)

More recently, the Association of Educational Psychologists (AEP) has felt the threat of LMS. The AEP's claim that 'current services could fall like dominos' is perhaps overstated. However, their fear that 'with financial constraints becoming worse, local authorities will increasingly look for savings in services or just 'wash their hands' of the problem through delegation' is realistic (Baumber, 1990).

The agency approach is certainly in vogue with government. However, policy makers at all levels would be mistaken to view it as a simple solution to the complex problems of improving the responsiveness and efficiency of public services. In constraining the range of services that LEAs can provide centrally and pushing the pace of delegation, the DES underestimate the negative impact such radical changes could have. The cynical view is that maximum delegation is designed to undermine the role of local government in directing educational policy, while still leaving the LEA tier in place to absorb criticism.

Authorities must be aware that by delegating resources they lose the ability to guarantee standards of provision and access to services for all children. They also rely heavily on the formula — which is discussed in detail below — through which delegated funds are allocated. It is an extremely crude device which may not allocate to schools their fair share of resources.

Lastly, heads and governors will require substantial training. Maximum delegation tacitly confers great responsibilities upon them. It requires that each school devise and put into effect its own policy on special needs including the school's policy towards buying agency support. This is also discussed in greater detail in the section on local management.

Formula Funding

'Needs based formula funding' is the main plank of resource allocation under LMS. It changes the way all mainstream school budgets are calculated and significantly alters LEA funding of special needs. In particular, the discretion of education officers has been ruled out as a method of allocating extra staff and resources to schools where the needs are greatest. A small number of studies have already described LEA approaches to funding special needs under LMS (Evans & Lunt, 1990; Lee, 1990a, 1990b) and others have looked at special needs funding as part of more general analyses (Lee, 1990c; Needham & Williams, 1989; Thomas, 1990). These studies show that LEAs each have a unique way of responding to special needs, but also that many rely on similar data to guide their allocation of resources — free school meal numbers. The aim here is to build on this earlier descriptive work, exploring problems in the formula funding policy and the way it has been implemented by LEAs in 1990/91.

Definitions

Surveys of the 1990 round of LMS schemes have shown that LEAs interpret special needs in many different ways. Consider the different ideas and considerable confusion highlighted by the following brief selection of definitions. Solihull, which is concerned with children with a 'learning difficulty', and Stockport where the focus is the needs of pupils in 'the least affluent parts of the Authority', offer definitions of special needs which are perhaps best described as reasonable but vague. Lancashire is one of a number of LEAs which seem to misunderstand Warnock's findings on the incidence of learning difficulties. The LEA states that 'pupils with non-statemented special needs will relate generally to pupils in the bottom 20% of the ability range'. Somerset LEA seems to target a far larger group of pupils. It allocates money to schools according to 'social needs and pupil intake of below-average ability' (the latter referring to half the pupil population presumably).

Social policy research shows that the definition of needs is a crucial landmark in any policy process aiming to allocate resources equitably between rivals. Notably, the definition should isolate the nature of the need in question and whether policy should address the needs of individuals, groups, institutions, communities or areas. A confusion over the different levels at which needs can be measured marred the educational priority area (EPA) policy recommended by the Plowden (1967) Report. Plowden talked of favouring '*schools* in *neighbourhoods* where *children* are most severely handicapped by *home* conditions' (Plowden, 1967: para. 174) (italics added).

The definition of need should play at least some part in determining the methods of its measurement. For example, the work of Barnes & Lucas (1974) shows that policies which aim to help individual children in need but which measure the needs of schools are fundamentally flawed. Their analysis of the inner London EPA concluded that the majority of needy children did not attend the most needy schools and that the majority of children in the most disadvantaged schools were not themselves in need (Barnes & Lucas, 1974: 89).

The definition is also a vital reference point at all stages of evaluation: assessing the merits of different indicators which might be used to measure needs; appraising how closely the adopted method matches resources to needs; or judging the policy's success by reference to outcomes. Evaluation is hindered in many areas where LEAs have fallen into the trap of 'definition by default' (Edwards, 1985: 23). In this way needs become defined in terms of variations in indicator readings and not variations in the conditions which the indicators are being used to pick up. For example, Doncaster LEA states that resources for special needs are targeted on 'schools where the percentage of pupils entitled to free meals justifies it'. This may be just a slip of the pen. However, policy makers must be aware that free school meal numbers justify nothing in themselves. A misunderstanding of the nature of social indicators is evident. Social indicators are used as convenient proxies for true measurements of need. They offer some sort of 'quick dial reading' of a situation without incurring the costs, methodological problems and risk of stigmatising people which are typical of more direct methods (Shonfield & Shaw, 1972: ix). The danger of definition by default is that an allocation may be extremely efficient in matching resources to indicator readings but inefficient in matching resources to needs or vary in its correlation with needs. The incidence of free meals in schools is particularly susceptible to changes in the rules governing entitlement to social security. In 1988 entitlement to free school meals was withdrawn from low paid working families (recipients of Family Credit). The effects of this were extremely varied. Free meal numbers remained constant in some schools but were drastically reduced in others. Yet it is obvious that the educational conditions had not changed in these schools.

Of course, it is argued that LEAs operate in the real world and that academic research takes place in ivory towers. It is pointed out that in choosing how to measure needs, the availability and administrative burden of different types of data are important practical considerations for LEAs. This in part helps to explain the popular use of free school meals to indicate special needs. It is readily available and cheap, regularly updated, provides easy comparisons between schools and is school-specific. It is also a form of data which has been widely used by LEAs to provide a basis for allocating extra staffing. However, familiarity may breed contempt: 'with familiar data we run into a . . . danger of over-confidence, forgetting that the observations themselves are not the concepts that they have been chosen to represent' (Bauer, 1966: 35). Indeed many governors and parents and various campaigning groups have challenged the use of free meal numbers to allocate resources under LMS. They see no reason to believe that social security entitlement is correlated with educational need and often refer to the Warnock

Report (DES, 1978b) for backing. However, Warnock and the 1981 Act are also cited by LEAs to justify their methods. The Leeds scheme states that 'The 1981 Act refers to some 20 percent of pupils having special educational needs' and claims that 'There is a correlation between such needs and the eligibility of pupils for free school meals'. Other LEAs rely on what might be called mutual justification. Warwickshire, for example, has

> accepted the findings of other Authorities and has recognised aspects of social deprivation as providing broad and consistent identification of pupils with learning difficulties. The provision of free school meals is a key determinant and this will be the basis of the LEA's measure for the time being.

What the exact correlation between needs and free meal numbers is, and whether it holds constant between LEAs, are matters which both require research. There is much to suggest, however, that the assumption which underlies mutual justification is severely flawed.

Simplicity and objectivity

The popularity of free meal data for measuring special needs is partly explained by its availability, but also because it fulfils DES rules about the nature of data to be used in LEA funding formulae.

The first is the simplicity rule. Formula funding is intended to make resource allocation more widely understood. The formula must be 'simple, clear and predictable' so that 'governors, headteachers, parents and the community can understand how it operates and why it yields the results it does' (DES, 1988: para. 104). Commendable as this aim is, it demands that LEAs adopt simple solutions to what are inherently extremely complicated problems. Complex, individualised measurements of need, such as that formerly used by the Inner London Education Authority (ILEA) in their educational priority index (EPI), are outlawed in favour of crude assessments based on indicator readings. The EPI recognised a key aspect of children's needs — the impact of multiple disadvantages. Disadvantage is not additive in any simple sense, although it is cumulative, as shown in Table 7.1

Without collecting data on a wide range of social and educational factors, surveying at least a representative sample of individual children in each school, and employing relatively complex statistical analyses, the effects of multiple disadvantage cannot be recognised by LEAs in formula funding. It is ironic therefore that critics of the ILEA method argued that compared to the EPI 'In order to bring discriminatory help to disadvantaged or needy children

TABLE 7.1 *Percentages of secondary pupils with different combinations of characteristics in verbal reasoning band 3*

Combination of characteristics	% pupils in VR band 3
No factors	10.8
Free meals only	21.1
Large families only	13.0
Social class only	18.4
Free meals, social class and large families	31.8

(Source: ILEA, 1982: 9, 11)

. . . policies . . . need to become substantially more complex' (Barnes & Lucas, 1974: 91). The government has treated greater simplicity as a 'nil-cost' improvement on past arrangements which, it is agreed, were generally mysterious and incomprehensible to all but a chosen few in each LEA. However, while a wider public appreciation of how school budgets are calculated is desirable, simplicity at the expense of equity is indefensible, especially where resources are scarce.

The second rule is that of objectivity. The stipulation is that LEAs must base their allocation on schools' 'objective needs'. The government's argument is that equity is protected by removing discretionary decisions and 'self-reporting' from the resource allocation process. Schools might otherwise be tempted to over-inflate their demands, and officers' judgements might be swayed by persuasive heads or personal preferences. It is claimed that an objective approach ensures 'an equitable allocation of the available resources' (DES, 1988a: para. 99). Contrary to this assertion, and to some extent contrary to logic, the push for objectivity may also have the opposite effect of limiting equity between institutions. The distinction which the DES makes between objective and subjective data provides the key to understanding why this might be. The crucial test appears to be whether or not data can be collected without involving any aspect of judgement by heads, teachers, educational psychologists or any other education authority staff. Many LEAs have fallen foul of the objectivity rule in attempting to use either schools' self-reported data on the incidence of needs or the assessments of psychologists or other specialist advisers. Kent LEA, for example, attempted to base special needs funding on a special educational needs audit conducted by school special educational needs (SEN) co-ordinators and headteachers. This was deemed too subjective by the DES. In a similar vein, a number of London LEAs believed it important to recognise the numbers of pupils at different levels of fluency in English when calculating school budgets. Such assessments were disallowed for being too judgemental. That all decisions over the allocation of resources rely on the judgements of someone or other in central government, education committees or LEA policy-making teams is not recognised.

In cases such as these the objectivity rule has perverse consequences. Free school meal data is deemed admissible regardless of how accurately, if at all, it can identify pupils' needs whereas professional assessments are disallowed regardless of their potential. Children's language needs — which vary along a continuum — can be measured only in terms of whether or not the child is a 'beginner in English' and not by assessing their level of fluency. The DES obviously see the first as an objective decision, the latter arbitrary. 'Objectively' the distinction is less than obvious or clear-cut.

If formula funding is to become truly 'needs-based' the pros and cons of enforcing simplicity and such a peculiar definition of objectivity on LEA practice must be reconsidered.

Misunderstanding the nature of special needs

Much of the above discussion lends weight to the argument that LMS is informed by a set of values at odds with other areas of education policy, especially policy on special educational needs. In particular LMS is built on a misunderstanding of the nature of special needs. Contrast the assumptions implicit in LMS with those of a DES circular specifically dealing with provision for pupils with learning difficulties. The objectivity and simplicity rules of LMS imply that needs exist apart from the policy maker's perception of them, are easily identified and measured, and that needs are not context-specific. On this, DES Circular 22/89 disagrees:

> When it is thought that a child may need special educational provision . . . the feelings and perceptions of the child concerned should be taken into account . . . The extent to which a learning difficulty hinders a child's development does not depend solely on the nature and extent of that difficulty. Other significant factors include the personal resources and attributes of the child as well as the help and support provided at home, and the provision made by the school and the LEA and other statutory and voluntary agencies. A child's special educational needs are thus related both to abilities and disabilities, and to the nature and extent of the interaction of these with his or her environment. (DES, 1989: para. 17)

If needs are context specific and defined as much by the response of the school as by the abilities and difficulties of the child, as Circular 22/89 suggests, LEAs will not be able to measure them by uniform methods across all schools. Given that there is a 'school effect' to be considered (Rutter *et al.*, 1979; Smith & Tomlinson, 1989) there is clearly a possibility that in allocating extra resources to schools which show a high incidence of children with learning difficulties, 'good' schools where children's needs are effectively responded to in a proactive way may be discriminated against financially. Many LEAs already use the results — typically the numbers of 'low scores' — for authority-wide tests to base their special needs allocation. These include data on verbal reasoning and reading ability, for IQ and mathematics tests, and even of the incidence of exam failure. In the future, data gathered from the Standard Assessment Tests (SATs) may be widely used. Such methods are all open to the criticism that they may provide financial rewards for inefficient schools and ineffective teaching practice. The fact that they are accepted by DES suggests that the nature of special educational needs is misunderstood by those directing LMS policy.

Pupil-led funding

The ability of LEAs to achieve an equitable system of funding is also limited by the emphasis the Government has placed on pupil-led funding. Pupil numbers adjusted for age differences, as the 'central determinant' of school's needs (DES, 1988a: para. 104c), must determine at least 75% of formula funding initially. From April 1993 the minimum is 80%. A maximum of 25% at present and 20% in future is all that remains to compensate schools for all other differences arising between them.

LEAs covering the most disadvantaged inner city areas are particularly restricted by these demands. These authorities typically serve extremely diverse communities. Pockets both of affluence and extreme deprivation are found within their boundaries. The range of conditions is sometimes extremely wide. Table 7.2 shows how the incidence of various social and educational factors — which may be related to pupil needs, underachievement or extra costs incurred by schools — vary between schools in an inner-London authority.

A school where over a third of pupils show disturbed behaviour obviously requires substantially more staff than another school where there are no such pupils. The need for extra teachers in a school where two-thirds of pupils require additional support in developing a fluency in English is great compared to a school where less than 2% of pupils have such needs. However, the formula is unable to recognise such vast differences. Where the

TABLE 7.2 *Differences in the incidence of social and educational factors in primary (P) and secondary (S) Schools in an Inner London LEA 1990*

Factor		LEA Average	Range Minimum	Maximum
Disturbed	(P)	22.3	0.0	42.3
behaviour	(S)	14.7	4.9	31.4
Non-Fluency	(P)	23.7	1.7	58.9
in English	(S)	19.2	0.3	32.2
Free school	(P)	51.9	16.9	78.6
Meals	(S)	47.7	25.0	61.6
Pupil	(P)	9.6	0.6	21.1
mobility	(S)	9.7	1.8	23.4

characteristics of pupils in different schools vary so greatly, a concentration on pupil numbers rather than pupil needs cannot yield a fair system of funding. There is a strong argument, as yet dismissed by the government, that in setting limits on the maximum LEAs can retain for central spending and the minimum they must devote to pupil-led funding, more leeway should be allowed for inner-city LEAs.

Meeting individual needs via the formula?

A final point of criticism is that the DES appear to be spreading confusion regarding the capacity of formula funding to meet individual pupils' needs. Paragraph 12 of *Assessments and Statements of Special Educational Needs*, DES Circular 22/89, states that

> Under local management schemes LEAs will have discretion as to whether or not they delegate provision for pupils with statements of SEN in ordinary schools and special units.

However, the paragraph continues:

> Where such provision is delegated the formula . . . must take account of the need to channel resources to meet the particular needs of pupils in such schools. (DES, 1989: para. 12)

Funding of special units via the formula already goes on. Lincolnshire LEA has a system which allocates allowances for each pupil attending a unit and these sums vary according to the type of facility and whether they are attached to primary or secondary schools.

In terms of allocating funding for statemented pupils what the formula can do falls far short of the ideal. It cannot respond to 'particular needs' as the circular proposes. Calculations of needs have to be based on (simple and objective) social or educational indicator readings, not specific measurements of need. Formulae cannot provide schools with funds tailored to the individual needs of certain pupils. Schools might receive a flat rate sum over and above the amount they receive per pupil to cover each statemented pupil. However, even with a range of lump sums, graded according to the child's need for extra teacher or support time, it would be difficult to adequately cover all statemented needs, the costs of which vary from next to nothing to many thousands of pounds per annum.

The government has many high aims for formula funding, most of which are laudable. Equal opportunities are promoted by fairness in resource allocation, predictability is a vital aid to the school manager, and clarifying who gets what and why is an essential part of enhancing accountability. However there are inherent faults with formula funding in its present form, and the government and LEAs to some extent have been mischievous to imply that it can operate in ways which it cannot.

Local Management

A key aspect in the evolution of LMS is that, as delegation gathers pace, the school will increasingly determine special education provision for its pupils. 'It will be for the school to consider how best to deploy its overall resources in order to offer the necessary provision' (DES, 1989: para. 12).

Giving schools a greater part of the education budget and untying the hands of governing bodies in the arrangement of provision may have many positive effects for all pupils. However, there is always a danger that special needs pupils will be treated like Cinderella, not least because they are typically in a minority and because they may be seen as a liability regarding the schools record of achievement as shown up by SATs testing each year. Worries about protecting provision for special needs are compounded because heads and governors have complete discretion over spending within their delegated budget. Even if the formula allocates each school a sum for special educational needs and/or social disadvantage there are no restrictions on how schools must spend that money. Many schools are in financial trouble because they have higher staffing costs than the average for their authority. It is both possible and probable that in such circumstances the retention of existing staff may take precedence over buying in extra support for special needs.

LMS does not allow governors to escape their responsibilities as laid down in the 1981 Act. They must still designate a member of the governing body to bear the responsibility for special needs issues. One of their duties must be to evaluate and report how effectively resources targeted for special needs are being used. LEAs must also monitor, but must be aware that financial accounting procedures are unlikely to provide such information. However, LMS does confuse the role of those managing schools. On the one hand there is an emphasis on governors' continuing responsibilities. At the same time, however, there is the introduction of competition via open enrolment, opting out and the SATs. Governors are being encouraged to see other schools as rivals and to view their own pupils in terms of cost and value. Evidence suggests that these latter messages are already affecting governors' decisions, for example in referrals for statements and even admissions policy. Coopers & Lybrand (1988: para. 2.65) hinted that unless special needs were well resourced via the formula schools might be encouraged to limit the numbers of pupils with learning difficulties which they admit. It is the increase in demands for statementing which has been most noticeable however. In the 18 months leading up to September 1990, Sheffield LEA saw a 56% increase in requests for pupils to be assessed. In Rotherham in the 12 months prior to September 1990 there was a 40% rise (Pyke, 1990). Such increases obviously place educational psychology services under great strain, cause delay in the assessment of children and issue of statements, place greater strain on central LEA budgets, and may encourage regressive attitudes towards special needs. LMS encourages the labelling of children and a reversal of the Warnock doctrine.

For schools the statement may fulfil a number of functions. It is a way of securing necessary provision for a pupil with learning difficulties. Indeed, under LMS it may be the only way LEAs can protect such provision from virement. Less admirably, the statement may be thought of by schools as a way of gaining, say, extra teaching support which can be deployed according to the school's priorities as opposed to individual pupil's needs. How schools will respond to their new role in determining special needs provision must be both a major concern to parents and, hopefully, to researchers.

Conclusion

The local management of schools policy is intended to bring benefits for schools and pupils. However, fears about the effects of LMS and formula funding are growing rather than being calmed. The evolution of the policy will make its impact clearer, but some negative consequences for pupils with learning difficulties and problems in funding special needs are already evident. These negative aspects have been highlighted. The starting point of the discussion was not a 'golden image' of the past, indeed the temptation to overestimate the fairness of traditional practice must be resisted. However, in the face of overwhelming government optimism about LMS, criticism has an important function. The underlying theme has been that LMS proposes simple solutions to complex problems in the allocation of resources, planning of provision and protection of pupils with special needs. Maximum delegation ensures that the central budgets of LEAs are pruned and that schools achieve greater autonomy. But it creates its own difficulties. It is likely that service provision will fragment. The rules governing LEA resource allocation formulae are shown by research to be naïve. Simple methods ensure rough justice in the distribution of resources between schools. The rules governing the acceptability of different forms of data mean that the impact of special needs is either partly ignored or imprecisely measured. Lastly, the crude assumption that local autonomy inherently yields greater responsiveness to pupils' needs ignores the complexity of the situation in which local managers are placed, the rival demands made on them and the perverse incentives created by LMS and other policies of the Education Reform Act. LEA officers and academics, politicians and parents, campaigning and advisory groups, teachers and governors, must all recognise and seek to address these problems if LMS is to be less of a 'major challenge' and more of a 'major opportunity' (DES, 1988a: para. 9) to pupils with special needs in our education system.

Acknowledgement

This research was funded by the ESRC, grant number R000 232504.

8 The LEA and its Schools: The Decentralised Organisation and the Internal Market[1]

ROSALIND LEVAČIĆ

As is well known, the 1988 Education Reform Act (ERA) was intended to open up the maintained school sector to market forces. It has done this in a number of ways: local management of schools (LMS), with pupil-driven formula funding and delegation to schools of budgets previously spent on central LEA services, and the creation of grant maintained (GM) schools and city technology colleges (CTCs). In this chapter I wish to consider in what ways these changes can be analysed as bringing about an 'internal market' and what is meant by this term. I shall present the internal market as one of three models for achieving internal co-ordination within an organisation, in contrast to the market proper which is a mode of external co-ordination between organisations. I shall argue that the internal market is best conceived as a device for securing management control within an organisation so as to deliver the organisation's goals more effectively. In relation to the post-ERA school system, the internal market model is applicable to the LEA and its schools, rather than to the system as a whole. The model of the internal market as an organisational device for securing management control in education is illustrated with a case study of a school district in Canada, Edmonton Public Schools, which over the last 14 years has evolved a system of decentralised control relying extensively on establishing internal markets. The case study is based on material gathered on a week's study tour of Edmonton Public School District in October 1990.[2] The most striking finding the study group came away with was the idea that decentralisation can be used to secure more effective control by headquarter's management than a highly centralised system of direct control of resources and processes in the schools. Though LMS in England and Wales is bringing about a weaker version of the internal market than the Edmonton example, it is still useful both as a reference point for analysing different LEA approaches and as a model for those LEAs wishing to exert control through setting policies and funding for schools and evaluating the resulting educational outcomes.

External Markets and Internal Hierarchies

The central question addressed in the literature is 'what method of co-ordination is "best" for organising a specified type of activity?' Modern economics literature on this question originates with Coase (1937) who sought to answer the question as to why some activities are undertaken by separate firms (i.e. production units) and co-ordinated by markets and why some are co-ordinated within the firm. However, the economic analysis of the internal co-ordination mechanisms of firms (and to a lesser extent other organisations) did not develop in a major way until Williamson's (1975) important book *Markets and Hierarchies*, followed by (1985) *The Economic Institutions of Capitalism*, which both build on Coase's initial insights. Williamson (1975) terms the co-ordination undertaken within a firm or organisation 'hierarchy' in contrast to market co-ordination which takes place between firms.

The Coase–Williamson approach singles out three main factors which, in conjunction, explain why in specific instances internal (hierarchical) co-ordination is more efficient (i.e. less costly) than market co-ordination. These are:

(1) *Bounded rationality.* Decision makers do not have complete information and are limited in their capacity to process it. Furthermore, information is not equally distributed: one party to a transaction often has more information about it than the other party and can exploit this 'information assymetry' for personal gain. If the parties to a contract have insufficient information to specify a market contract that will work satisfactorily as future events unfold and the unexpected occurs, then internal co-ordination is more effective because it provides for greater flexibility in changing the nature of the tasks as new information becomes available.

(2) *Opportunism.* This is the guileful pursuit of self-interest. Such behaviour means that parties to market contracts will try to take advantage at the expense of the other party of any loopholes in the contract, which are ultimately due to information assymetry and bounded rationality.

(3) *Asset specificity.* This occurs when a firm produces goods or services using highly specific resources which have few alternative uses except to supply the purchaser to whom the firm has contracted to supply. If the market contract breaks down then both parties will find it costly to find a new

partner for exchange. This condition, combined with imperfect information and opportunism, makes market co-ordination more risky and costly than internal co-ordination.

Modes of Internal Co-ordination

Following Williamson, the literature has used the term 'hierarchy' as a label for internal co-ordination in contrast to market co-ordination between independent organisations. While such a label is convenient, 'hierarchy' is an unfortunate term to have used since it does not help in discriminating between different forms of internal co-ordination — the issue which is the focus of this paper. From scanning a wide range of social science literature it seems appropriate to distinguish three main modes of internal coordination.[3]

(1) *Hierarchy*. Authority is concentrated at the apex of a pyramidal structure of superordinates and subordinates and delegated downwards through a clearly defined command structure which is regulated by tightly specified and detailed rules. Co-ordination occurs vertically through rules and commands.

(2) *Network*. This is an interlinkage of individuals or organisational units which operates both formally, as through common interest associations, or informally through social contacts. Information and favours are exchanged and agreements made to undertake concerted actions. The dominant mode of co-ordination consists of informal agreement and implicit exchange.

Within the broad category of networking one can include organisational culture and professionalism. Both offer a means for combating opportunism by inducing employees to behave in ways which are in the interests of the organisation (as defined by top management) or of the organisation's clients.

(3) *Internal market*. The market form of co-ordination in which agents voluntarily exchange goods and services at a price is mimicked within an organisation. Units within an organisation act as buyers and sellers and exchange services or goods with each other at a price. A form of competition is created by ensuring that the buyer and selling units have alternative exchange partners, i.e. there is not a monopoly or monopsony.

This theoretical framework for analysing external co-ordination between organisations and internal co-ordination within an organisation is summarised in Figure 8.1. Each oval represents an organisation which is externally co-ordinated by markets. Each organisation is internally co-ordinated by one or more of the three modes of internal co-ordination — hierarchy, networks or internal markets.[4] A crucial dimension of an organisation's internal structure is its location along the centralised/decentralised continuum. Brown (1990: 36) offers a useful definition of decentralisation: 'Decentralisation is the extent to which authority to make decisions is distributed among the roles in an organisation.' Thus there is a direct relationship between centralisation and a high degree of hierarchy. Internal markets, where sub-units are free to trade with each other or with external organisations, are a feature of decentralised organisations. Networks within an organisation facilitate and oil the operations of both hierarchical and internal market co-ordination.

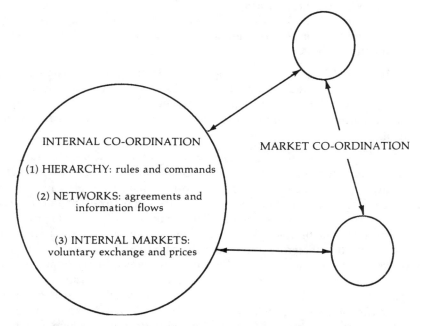

FIGURE 8.1 *The external and internal co-ordination of organisations*

Application of the Model to the State Schools Sector

In applying this analysis of organisational structure to the changes in the schooling system brought about by the 1988 Act, we need to specify (as Keep (1992, this volume) points out) the appropriate place to draw the organisation's boundaries. There are three possibilities:

(1) The DES is the HQ of education enterprises, the LEAs are its divisions running lots of school outlets. An internal market is formed by creating

GM schools and CTCs as well as by fostering competition between maintained schools. So, in Figure 8.1, if the small ovals represent a GM school and a CTC, the boundary would be drawn around all the organisations.

(2) The organisational boundary is drawn around the LEA. In Figure 8.1 this would be the large oval. The GM schools and CTCs are out in the external marketplace just as are the independent schools. The internal market is the structure that governs the relationship between the LEA and its schools and could serve as an instrument of control through which the LEA seeks to attain its strategic objectives.

(3) Each state school is an organisational unit co-ordinated *vis-à-vis* the others by the market. This model would be apt if schools were funded through vouchers.

The second case is the most appropriate in current circumstances. The DES currently has less capability than the LEAs to set up control mechanisms other than those provided by market accountability and so is unlikely to demonstrate the use of internal markets as an instrument of organisational control.

It is important to distinguish external from internal markets because they offer different forms of control and accountability. An internal market is necessarily a highly regulated market and is managed precisely in order to achieve effective organisational control. It differs in many important respects from an external market. The main difference being the absence of any direct property rights in the profits generated by the sub-unit or the absence of profits at all. It is therefore quite inappropriate to offer a critique of internal markets based on criteria of good performance which apply to perfectly or workably competitive or contestable markets. The appropriate criteria for judging the performance of an internal market is whether it does provide a better means to securing organisational objectives given the key problems of limited information, bounded rationality and opportunism which have to be addressed.

The LEA as an Internal Market

Local management of schools has set up two kinds of internal market relationships depending on whether the schools or the centre are buyers or sellers.

Formula funding establishes the LEA as a buyer of education services from its schools. It has considerable discretion is setting the terms of the contract. Through the formula it determines the price it offers schools for educating a particular type of pupil and also the terms on which it will discriminate between schools on criteria of size, condition of the buildings and so on. Within the ceiling set by government the LEA decides which discretionary exceptions it will retain. So it has, for example, considerable powers to limit or stimulate competition between schools by the terms on which it provides free home to school transport. The LEA regulates the internal market by determining the number and types of schools, the categories of pupil they can admit particularly in terms of age and residence. There still remains considerable variety across LEAs in the terms on which they manage the internal market, as indicated in Thomas (1990).

Another area in which the LEA now acts as purchaser of services provided by schools is premises for community education provision. The LEA can require schools to accommodate community education taking place out of school hours and can decide the price it will pay. This has already led to considerable argument between schools and LEAs as to what constitutes community use and what are appropriate charges to compensate for the costs incurred as well as to problems with budgeting for community education which is not included in the GSB (*Education*, 1990b). The costs to the school may not be just the extra heating, wear and tear and caretaking, but the loss of more lucrative fees. For community education taking place on school premises within school hours the LEA is in a much weaker position and cannot legally insist on requisitioning space at a price fixed by itself. This is an example in the English and Welsh context where the LEAs have had certain regulatory features of the internal market determined for them by central government.

In the second set of internal market relationships the LEA acts as seller to the schools. Considerable pressure to do this has been placed on LEAs by Circular 7/88s (DES, 1988a) requirement that limited discretionary exceptions do not exceed 10%, and after four years 7%, of the general schools budget. Thomas (1990) reports that most LEAs expected in 1990/91 to be near the 10% limit. The Secretary of State for Education has also criticised LEAs for retaining too much of the GSB even though they are not breaking the ceiling for limited discretionary exceptions (*Education*, 1990a) and is expected to introduce a tighter limit for all discretionary exceptions. In a study of DES responses to the LEAs' 1989 LMS submissions currently being undertaken at the OU we have found that the principle of maximum delegation is one of the main issues pursued by the DES in requiring amendments to schemes. Thus LEAs are and will be forced by the current government, if not already doing it on their volition, to delegate budgets to schools for LEA provided services. The personnel currently providing such services will have to recoup the costs of their departments by selling their services to schools. The competitive tendering legislation is also putting pressure on LEAs to place their service departments on a commercial footing. However, centralised bulk contracting enabled many LEAs to specify contracts which their direct labour forces won. Once the transition period is over this will no longer be so easy as schools can exercise the option to tender elsewhere.

The services which will be structured within an internal market in which schools are purchasers include:

- buildings and ground maintenance
- equipment repair
- educational psychologists and welfare officers
- advisory teachers
- centrally based teachers, e.g. music and swimming provision
- library and museum services
- teacher and field centres
- technical and legal advice
- financial administration, e.g. pay roll.

Apart from county schools, GM schools are also likely to buy in LEA central services. Bush's (1990) study of two GM schools records that in their first year the two schools between them purchased from their ex-LEAs advice for probationers and on new curriculum developments, support for children with learning difficulties, inspection of some departments, cleaning, grounds maintenance and pay roll services.

The Rationale for Internal Markets as an Internal Control Mechanism

As already noted, a decentralised organisation is a necessary but not sufficient condition for internal markets. Thus the organisational rationale for internal markets must begin with that for decentralisation. Brooke (1986) argues that internal structure evolves in response to pressures for both centralisation and decentralisation. Organisations are observed to reverse their movement in either direction because the pressures for decentralisation and centralisation are ever present though varying in their relative intensity.

The advantages of centralisation are:

(1) directing scarce resources on the basis of organisation-wide information;
(2) pursuing the interests of the organisation as a whole as when, for example, restructuring and rationalisation are needed;
(3) providing a career structure for supporting head office interests.

Here one can see many of the arguments in favour of more LEA control of education: efficiency in central planning of the provision of schools and, as in the School Management Task Force (1990) report, a central LEA role in teacher professional development, staff training and headship succession policies.

The arguments Brooke (1986) puts forward in favour of decentralisation again have a familiar ring:

(1) reducing costs by devolving decision making;
(2) easing communication problems;
(3) more rapid decision making;
(4) local management is more in tune with local market conditions;
(5) local decision making improves the congruence between organisational goals set by HQ management and those of the organisation's employees, provided the latter are set appropriate targets and motivated by rewards and sanctions to attain them.

Posing these counter advantages against each other highlights the fundamental issue for organisational design which is where the knowledge required for making particular decisions is located within the organisation. According to Hayek's (e.g. 1989) conception of knowledge it has to be generated, communicated and acted upon. Centralisation is an inefficient means of co-ordination when the knowledge required for effective decision making is not possessed by HQ management — due to bounded rationality and because opportunistic subordinates have insufficient incentives to generate and communicate the required knowledge up the hierarchical chain. However, there may well be other areas of decision making which require an overall but less detailed knowledge of the organisation and its environment. Hence the balance struck between centralisation and decentralisation for effective organisational planning and control depends on the nature of the organisation's activities and the environment with which it interacts.

The restructuring of LEAs required by LMS has many of the same features as the move from the unitary form of firm organisation to the multidivisional form. A standard definition of these two forms is given by Cable (1988: 13).

U-form firms are functionally specialised, hierarchically arranged organisations . . . there is a single peak co-ordinator (a person or board of directors to whom are responsible the heads of specialist departments dealing with production, marketing, purchasing, finance, etc.). Within each functional area there may be several further horizontal layers of responsibility and vertical demarcations of more finely specialised tasks.

In the M-form firm, production activities are broken down into a number of quasi-autonomous operating divisions (typically . . . based on products, brands or geographic area). The activities are co-ordinated via a general office, assisted by an elite staff, which undertakes strategic planning and resource allocation among the divisions, and exercises a characteristic form of monitoring and control over them. The M-form may be distinguished . . . from the holding company firm which, though divisionalised, lacks the requisite general office functions.

Prior to LMS, LEAs were largely organised along U-form lines with separate functional departments for finance, property, personnel and so forth, as illustrated in Figure 8.2. Each of these functional departments provided services direct to schools, largely on terms decided at central office and any one school would deal with each department separately. The accounting system reported the costs of the central departments functions to schools as as group and not the costs of the individual school.

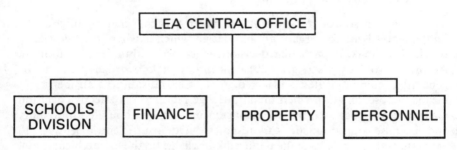

FIGURE 8.2 *Pre LMS: The LEA as a U-form organisation*

In contrast LMS has created an M-form type of LEA, as illustrated in Figure 8.3. Schools have become semi-autonomous operating units and the functional departments (such as property and technical services, personnel, supplies, financial administration) have had some of their functions transferred to schools, which are now treated as cost centres in the accounts. Many of the central functional departments have or will become sellers of their services to schools in competition with external suppliers.[5]

It is widely argued (as reported in Cable, 1988) that firms abandon the U-form in favour of the M-form as they become larger and operate in more complex and uncertain environments, because the M-form structure copes better with the problems of bounded rationality and opportunism. It does this by separating operational from strategic decision making. The former becomes the responsibility of the divisions leaving top level management to concentrate on strategic decision making. They can now do this more

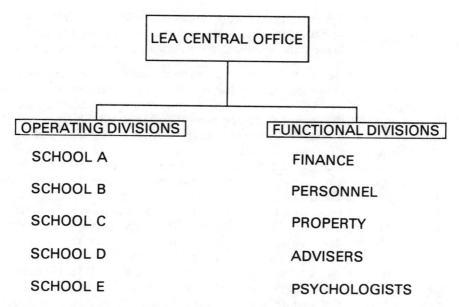

FIGURE 8.3 *LMS: The LEA as an M-form organisation*

effectively because they are not subject to information overload and poor communication channels which impede hierarchical managerial control in the U-form organisation. The opportunistic tendencies of middle managers are channelled to the fulfilment of organisational goals by setting them targets, monitoring outcomes and rewarding good performance. The M-form organisation is still relatively tightly controlled from the centre and so is not as decentralised as the holding company organisation. As Mintzberg (1979) notes, the M-form HQ management typically control:

- the definition and delineation of the divisions
- allocation of overall resources
- design of performance and control systems
- appointment and dismissal of divisional managers
- provision of certain support services.

Apart from the removal of LEA powers to appoint and dismiss headteachers and other teachers, all the other functions of HQ management are possessed by LEAs under LMS. Interestingly, Mintzberg considers the M-form unsuited to public service agencies like education authorities because of their inability to measure the achievement of their social goals and because the divisions (schools) are seldom divested.[6] He concludes therefore that public service agencies which have adopted M-form have to remain uncontrolled, or exert control through regulation of work process or by setting up 'artificial' targets. This argument provides a rationale for the national curriculum and its testing as an essential control mechanism for regulating internal markets.

Despite such reservations there has been a marked movement in a number of countries towards decentralisation and internal markets for public sector agencies (Caldwell, 1990). A major reason for this is to combine the claimed superior efficiency of market co-ordination compared to hierarchical administrative co-ordination with maintaining access to merit goods, such as education and health, regardless of income. A divisionalised organisation need not operate internal markets, but internal markets can function only in such an organisation. Internal markets are advocated as a mechanism for improving the performance of the divisions in serving the needs of the organisation. The term 'internal market' is used much more frequently in the context of the restructuring of the NHS than it is with respect to schools, where competition is stressed more. The proposal for internal markets for the NHS is usually attributed to Enthoven's adaptation of the idea from his work with health maintenance organisations in the USA (Enthoven, 1978, 1988). In the context of the NHS, 'internal markets are seen as a possible way of retaining a system of finance which secures the macro objectives of cost containment and equity, but incorporating within that system micro-incentives for efficiency and consumer satisfaction' (Bevan, 1989). Exactly the same justification applies to internal markets for educational provision.

The NHS internal market is to be created by making the district health authorities (DHAs) and budget-holding GPs purchasers of treatment on behalf of their patients from hospitals which may be within or outside their own district or run by NHS trusts or by private concerns. In theory, the incentive for efficiency (i.e. cost minimisation and effective service) comes from the competition between hospitals for the custom of GPs and DHAs who seeks out the best treatment for their patients within a budget constraint. As Mullen (1990) points out, this is only one of many variants of an internal market and one which allows the patient no direct choice of provider and no voice on the management boards. Thus the NHS internal market is a purely administrative device, unlike education where the customer can choose between providers and influence governing bodies. The rationale for these differences reflects the perception that a greater degree of expert knowledge is required to make medical decisions about one's personal health than about one's child's education! This is reflected in the greater power of the medical compared to the teaching professionals.

In essence then, internal markets are advocated as a way of resolving the problems of internal administrative co-ordination using hierarchies and networks. These problems arise from the basic factors of bounded rationality and opportunism. Hierarchical co-ordination gives senior managers inadequate information by which to regulate the activities of subordinates through rules and commands and insufficient incentives for opportunistic subordinates to behave in ways which promote the organisation's goals. As Nielsen, Peters & Hisrich (1985) note, organisations face the problem that the advantages of hierarchial co-ordination in integrating the activities of sub-units can conflict with the need for sub-units to be flexible and innovative in responding to a changing external environment. M-form gives divisions autonomy and flexibility but makes internal co-ordination of their activities more difficult. The solution advocated by Neilsen *et al.* is intrapreneurship whereby relatively small independent units within a large organisation create, test and expand improved or innovative services, technologies or methods which are purchased by other internal units. Intrapreneurship or internal markets[7] are seen as particularly suited to service or functional divisions.

Edmonton Public Schools: Tight Mission and Loose Means

In this chapter I have deliberately focused on the internal market as a form of organisational decentralisation and not as an aspect of political decentralisation. This is done in order to give a sharper focus by concentrating on one key aspect of internal markets. A good example of the use of internal markets as a managerial device is Edmonton Public Schools (EPS) where, as Brown (1990) confirms, political decentralisation does not feature: school councils with parent representation are set up at the principal's discretion and have an advisory role only. The creation of internal markets has been a deliberate strategy, evolved over the last 14 years, in order to secure better control by the board of trustees (nine persons elected by the taxpayers who support Edmonton Public Schools) and the Superintendent (the top appointed official).

The previous structure had been U-form *par excellence* with (from a UK perspective) extreme centralisation of functions organised around a planning, programming budgeting system. The curriculum subjects or programmes were run from the centre by 30 programme specialists or consultants (close to what we call advisers) who supplied schools directly with books and materials for teaching the curriculum as prescribed by the provincial government. Allocations for and appointments of support staff and teachers were made centrally. The function of school principal was to co-ordinate the resources provided by many disparate central officials and to represent staff and community views to board officials. The perceived problems of this system illustrate well the inadequacy of the U-form structure in coping with bounded rationality and opportunism:

> Elected trustees and senior administrators became increasingly aware of problems resulting from an organizational structure with 'blurred' lines of accountability, poor communications, and an absence of defined job expectations. Problems resulting from lack of staff identity and opportunity for meaningful involvement in and ownership of decisions were also increasing . . .
>
> Examples of schools receiving a mix of services that was difficult to rationalize were legion — new library texts but not the necessary accompanying shelving . . . (Smilanich, 1988: 1–2)

Decentralised budgeting was chosen as the means to initiate a fundamental restructuring of the organisation. From allowing schools to determine the spending of 2% of the education budget, 75% is now delegated.

> There was an underlying belief that the decentralisation of funds would establish the means and the framework which would enable the school and indirectly the classroom teacher maximum flexibility in meeting the varying needs of students. It was firmly believed that it was the quality of the teacher–pupil interaction at the classroom level that was crucial to the learning process and that it must not only be preserved but ever enhanced. With the increased opportunity for decisions at the school level provided in a climate of trust, more of the creative talents and potential of teachers could be released. . . . Empowerment of staff has become a district watch-word. (Smilanich, 1988: 1)

Since 1979 schools have been formula funded according to the number of pupils on roll on 30th September. The amount received per pupil depends on the pupils' characteristics. For incremental funding there is now only a slight premium for high school students over elementary ones and there are additional categories of high ability, second language programmes and various kinds of special need due to learning difficulties, physical handicap and behaviour problems. It is the board's policy to reduce the number of categories which have been cut over the ten years since 1980 from 22 to 13. There is a small non-pupil related supplement for size of school and social composition. The delegated budget covers all staff costs, materials, books and equipment. Staff are paid out of the school budget at the average district salary for their post. Utility costs are delegated to about 80% of schools which choose this. Maintenance has not yet been delegated because of opposition from the direct labour force. Eighteen out of the 192 schools have a delegated budget for consultants.

Parents can opt to send their children to out-of catchment schools but do not receive free transport if they do so. Forecasting pupil numbers for the start of the academic year in September, which is when the financial year now begins as well, is difficult. Schools experience unexpected fluctuations in their rolls, not just because of open boundaries but also because of population changes. When this occurs, the principal has to make quick adjustments to class organisation and staffing. Teachers who are surplus to requirements are quickly dismissed from the school but, unlike the situation in England and Wales since LMS, they are guaranteed employment by the district which requires schools with vacancies to take on redeployed teachers.

The continually reiterated management philosophy of the district is that the board and its officers are concerned with results not school processes. The district clearly states its objectives and has a strong line of management accountability passing from the Superintendent to six associate superintendents who are each responsible for about 30 school principals whom they hold accountable for the results in their school. It is a firm principle that each person should have only 'one boss'. The board and its officers object to proposals for school councils with power because this would blur the line of accountability and fatally weaken their management control system.

Board officials openly recognise that the process of monitoring and evaluating the performance of principals and their schools and holding principals accountable for their results is still imperfect and needs much further development. Still they have proceeded further than most education authorities. From 1980 schools have been assessed internally using data gathered from an annual attitude survey of its staff, pupils and parents. Since 1987 tests of pupils at grades 3, 6 and 9 have been used as well. These are written (not multiple choice) tests in language arts, maths, science and humanities. Their purpose is to evaluate the school, not the individual student. Schools are placed in bands according to the discrepancy between pupils' measured general ability and curriculum attainment. In order to devise the tests, the district has reformulated the Alberta provincial curriculum so that it is stated in terms of learning objectives rather than content and so is quite similar in form to the attainment targets of the English and Welsh national curriculum. The associate superintendants review annually with each of their principals his or her school's performance indicators measured by the tests and attitude surveys and also pupil recruitment. Areas for improvement are then agreed. These reviews should mesh in with the district annual planning cycle followed by each school. As part of the district budget planning process each school is notified in early spring of its budget for the next financial and academic year. The principal is responsible for involving staff and the community in a process of school management planning which determines school priorities, the ways in which resources will be deployed to achieve these and the resultant budget. Each school's plan and budget is reviewed in public by a subcommittee of three trustees and agreed. However, come September, the budget may need drastic reworking if forecast and actual pupil numbers differ substantially.

It is clearly district policy to ease out principals who perform badly on these criteria and the district is beginning to evolve a form of succession planning for principals. Favoured young deputies are selected to be 'principal at large', i.e. attached to the district and assigned to special projects. There appeared to be a strong organisational culture, reflected in catch phrases (tight mission: easy means; the golden rule is gold rules, celebrating growth) and a sense that to ascend the career ladder in the district it was necessary to fit in with that culture. Networks and cultural osmosis were used to reinforce the more overt control mechanisms of the internal market and its associated performance indicators.

The responses of EPS employees to the incentive system established through internal markets appear to be largely in accordance with predictions and provide examples of the expected benefits of internal markets as well as suggesting certain drawbacks.

There is evidence of flexibility and responsiveness to client demand. One particular success story, from Vic Composite High School, was cited as an example of an entrepreneurial principal who, over five years, created from a failing vocational school a magnet school for the performing and fine arts. Using income from growing student recruitment (including from the Far East) and private sector involvement enough money was generated for small building works, despite the absence of a delegated budget for building maintenance. In other schools there has been a growth in language programmes, especially in French immersion programmes. It was felt that schools had initiated the use of computers in learning much more effectively than if they had each been centrally allocated a fixed number of computers. Some schools had led the way with others then following, ensuring that if schools spent their own budgets on computers then they would be used by teachers.

There are examples of greater efficiency in resource use. Schools trade with each other; for instance, the expertise of a particular teacher is bought in either to teach students or to provide in-service training (INSET) for staff. It has been noted that schools which pay for their own utilities have cut their energy costs. There is no need for schools to hoard materials (a typical feature of central planning systems); some have sold redundant equipment to supplement school funds. Similarly, schools are now willing to rent out space for community users, whereas before they would claim to have no spare accommodation. Musical instrument repairs are done more cheaply by the private sector and the central service has now been wound up. There are now fewer underemployed teachers and greater pressure on poor performers to retrain or retire. However, there is concern to prevent principals charging parents for school services. Another concern was rising class sizes as teachers preferred to teach larger classes and have more non-contact time. In response to parental pressure an upper class size of 30 has now been imposed by the district in contravention of its own principle that the centre should not intervene in school processes but concentrate on evaluating results and requiring accountability.

Special needs is an interesting area where schools' services are purchased on behalf of clients by the district. All special needs pupils (including those who would be statemented in Britain) are funded with an enhanced grant the size of which depends on specified criteria. Board officials stated that the integration of special needs pupils in mainstream schools was proceeding well because schools are attracted by the additional non-earmarked money. This enables a school either to run smaller classes for mainstream pupils ('regular kids'), into which are integrated one or more special needs pupils, or to employ classroom support staff who work with all the children. To have the additional grant attached to him or her the pupil has to be professionally assessed. Some of the testing is done by schools and some by 'consultants' (i.e. educational psychologists) and this now makes up the bulk of consultancy services requested by schools. The market responsiveness of principals to special needs funding is notable. The number of assessed special needs children, including gifted children, has risen as has the percentage of the education budget being spent on special needs. Board officials are concerned that 'regular kids are getting squeezed' and have responded by reducing the number of special needs categories and capping special needs expenditure at 12% of the total budget which has reduced the special needs multiplier. So as principals increase the number of special needs children they, in effect, reduce the per capita grant enhancement.

A particularly interesting aspect of intrapreneurship concerns the role of the consultancy service. The consultants have experienced the most profound change of all. They have been deprived of much of the gold that rules. Under the old planning programming budgeting system the consultants were major budget holders determining the bulk of resources that went into schools. They then became a central service free to schools on request (largely for special needs assessments it turned out) or to be called on by associate superintendents wanting advice on a school. Under a pilot project 18 schools were given a budget for consultancy services to spend as they pleased. Edmonton consultancy services could be purchased at a 25% discount. Despite this, only 60% of the delegated consultancy budget was spent by schools on EPS consultancy services — 90% of this for assessing and programming special needs pupils. As these schools can choose which consultant to employ this provides an explicit market test of a consultant's performance. Even this limited exposure to the internal market was claimed to have brought about significant changes in the attitudes and mode of operation of consultants. Whereas they had been producer oriented — providing INSET courses which teachers did not find particularly useful, or determining the number of wooden puzzles and scissors to be issued to a kindergarten — they have become far more client and service oriented, offering over 70 types of service. The two-fold purpose of the consulting service is now stated as (a) to influence district direction, and (b) assist others in the attainment of results. Consulting is defined 'as a collaborative process that leads to the attainment of mutually shared objectives. The selection of the process rests with the participant responsible for the results' (Edmonton Public Schools, 1990). A survey of the consultancy service pilot project in 1989 found that 64% of school staff and 27% of consultancy staff 'perceived improvement in their ability to determine the nature and level of service, in the effectiveness and efficiency of the service provided and in the access, delivery and distribution of services' (Edmonton Public Schools, 1989). At the time visited (October 1990) the district was in the midst of gearing up to decide whether and how to extend the pilot project. This was evidently the culmination of many years' careful internal political manouevring by those officials favouring delegation who had faced considerable resistance from consultants feeling threatened by the prospect of having to sell their services to schools. The favoured solution appeared to be to keep back part of the budget for centrally determined activities and to delegate the rest to schools on a voluntary basis, using pressure from schools as a leverage to secure more delegation.

The Edmonton case also illustrates a number of potential drawbacks to internal markets. A major unresolved issue is the extent to which surrogate market performance indicators can be constructed and applied so as to ensure desirable performance by divisional managers and their units. Though now applied for four years, the Edmonton tests are still being developed further and modified. How well they indicate the effectiveness with which resources have been utilised in the education of individual children remains problematic. There are still areas of performance where no information is collected, such as the progress of special needs pupils and the attainments and destinations of students leaving school at 16.

A key problem with any market solution is how well a market contract can be specified so that it gives appropriate incentives for the participants to promote the organisation's goals. The superiority of Williamson's hierarchical co-ordination is that it does not require the specification of contracts, but enables activities to be adjusted by means of commands. An internal market contract requires the purchaser to specify what the seller must do for the price charged. Pupil-driven formula funding is an example of such a contract. Much effort is expended determining the appropriate sum of money needed to educate pupils with specific characteristics. Special needs are a particularly good example of the problems associated with drawing up a financial contract. In the face of what is in part opportunistic behaviour by principals, the district has continually revised the terms of the contract. The district has not got anywhere near to resolving the problem of how to monitor the special needs contract. At least the specification of the contract for educating pupils is less informationally demanding than a health service contract where the number of contingencies is much greater and the cost of specific treatments is more difficult to determine. A further problem with contract specification is ensuring that perverse incentives are not created which cause opportunistic employees to act against the interests of the organisation. In the Edmonton case, the increase in class size and additional school charges, were both regarded by board officials as undesirable opportunistic behaviour which they sought to eradicate by recourse to rules. These are examples of the unease frequently expressed concerning the use of financial criteria in making decisions about the allocation of resources for merit goods. However, financial and economic cost criteria are going to be applied at some level in the political process of resource allocation, so the issue must be about whether there are decision-making locations where economic criteria should not be taken into account.

Another problem with internal market contracts is that they generate uncertainty about income and resource flows. If pupil numbers unexpectedly fall school plans have to be speedily revised. However, hierarchical co-ordination has its own uncertainties, such as unreliability of supply which leads to hoarding.

Internal markets for public services are criticised for accentuating differentiation in the quality of provision. While it was made clear that Edmonton schools varied widely in their characteristics and that some performed relatively badly, at board level there appeared little concern about inequity caused by internal markets for schools. Senior officials and the chairwoman of the board seemed convinced that decentralised resource management combined with tight central control over goals and results improved general performance by weeding out the incompetent and raising standards overall. A speedy response to failing schools which could be mobilised by a district with strong line management accountability would limit the damage to pupils. (According to a board officer, three out of ten principals have the ability to turn a school round and 'can be sent in to rescue a failing franchise'.)

Conclusion

Edmonton Public Schools illustrates well the theme of this paper — that internal markets are an organisational device for securing better management control and thereby attaining organisational goals more effectively than can alternative alternative modes of co-ordination. Used in this way internal markets have to be judged according to how well they resolve the organisational problems posed by bounded rationality and opportunism. Internal markets, as used in Edmonton, are seen by central managers and policy setters as providing a better solution to these problems than centralisation. There is considerable emphasis on central managers concentrating on securing and using the right information for directing and controlling the organisation and providing principals, and through them teachers, with an appropriate set of incentives and powers to promote the educational aims of the district. The element that makes local management of schools crucially different from the Edmonton system is the strong force for political decentralisation in the legislation. While internal markets as an aspect of administrative decentralisation have to be justified as being a more effective co-ordination mechanism than alternatives, political decentralisation, with its diffusion of power, is an end in itself.

However, political decentralisation makes for blurred lines of account-ability and so makes it more difficult to implement a strong central controlling force as in Edmonton. Furthermore, most LEAs have had internal markets imposed upon them and many have still to work out their new role. Nevertheless, the Edmonton case has much to offer as a model of how a decentralised structure with internal markets still offers a strong management control role for an LEA through its resource setting and evaluation functions.

Acknowledgements

I would like to thank Tony Bush for his helpful comments and Sasha Rebmann for executing the diagrams. All remaining errors or lack of clarity are my responsibility.

Notes

1. Revised version of a paper given to the British Education Research Association symposium on Local Management of Schools, Derbyshire College of Higher Education, November 1990.
2. The study tour was organised by Cambridge Education Associates in conjunction with Edmonton Public Schools. Key postholders (district officers, board trustees, teachers, and one parent) gave presentations and answered questions, documents were made freely available and three schools were visited.
3. An Open University course, currently in production (D212, Running the Country) is organised around a theoretical framework of three main modes of co-ordination — hierarchy, market and networks.
4. Organisations can also be externally co-ordinated by network and hierarchy. The 1988 Education Act reflects a strengthening of hierarchy as a mode of co-ordination used by the DES in relation to LEAs and schools and a decline in the influence of policy networks.
5. In addition, competitive tendering legislation has required central service departments to tender for a market contract.
6. The fate of schools which persistently fail to keep within their budgets under LMS has yet to be experienced.
7. Whether intrapreneurship means precisely the same as internal markets is not clear from the literature. I would suggest that intrapreneurship is a particular form of internal market where divisions trade with each other, whereas internal markets include the organisation's HQ 'purchasing' services from other divisions by means of various kinds of contract.
8. Associate superintendant, Edmonton Public Schools, Alberta.

9 Schools in the Marketplace? — Some Problems with Private Sector Models

EWART KEEP

Secondary schools and larger primaries will have to adjust to a new management culture under LMS. Heads will become, in effect, managing directors responsible for the way their schools perform. Parents will become shareholders. (Hugill, 1989)

Introduction

The Government's education reforms reflect, among other things, a belief that markets and private sector management techniques can help provide answers to the perceived problems and deficiencies of the public sector, and that their imposition on schools will result in improvements in standards of provision. The introduction of local management of schools (LMS), linked to open enrolment and enhanced parental power, serves as an example of attempts to create competition and build a market culture in the public sector.

One result of these developments has been burgeoning interest within the education world in private sector management techniques. Numerous books and articles on the management of schools have appeared, many of which lay stress on what teachers can learn from private sector management practice (see, for example, Everard, 1986; Poster & Day, 1988). At another level, one of the underlying motivations for much of the school/industry liaison activity in the UK, has been the belief that schools staff can, through the process of closer links with private sector business, and particularly through periods of secondment to companies, gain experience of management techniques that can then be translated back into their schools.

Not everyone has reacted with unqualified enthusiasm to these developments (see, for example, Holt, 1987; Torrington & Weightman, 1983), and Margaret Maden, the chief education officer of Warwickshire has suggested that, 'the zeal with which some commentators and politicians try to foist the managerial model of big business on to the education service has to be scrutinized' (Maden, 1989). The purpose of this paper is simply to raise a few questions about some of the more simplistic attempts to equate schools with businesses, and to underline the fact that there is a need for caution in trying to borrow managerial techniques from private sector organisations. In terms of structure, the operation of markets is examined first, followed by a discussion of the diversity of private sector management techniques. Finally, some of the fundamental differences between schools and businesses are underlined.

Models of Market-based Competition

One of the most important points of departure for the Government's education reforms, has been their belief in the need to introduce the discipline of market-based competition into the state school system (Thomas, 1988; Sterne, 1987; Brighouse, 1988a). Various ministerial statements make it clear that it is envisaged that schools should be engaged in more or less unrestricted competition with one another. The aim of this competition, based on opting out, open enrolment and local management of schools, is both to make schools more responsive to the wishes of parents, and also to 'expose inefficient schools' (Sutcliffe, 1989). As Duffy (1990) puts it, 'LMS is about putting schools into the market-place, and the hard discipline of the market-place is that the weak go to the wall'.

This Social Darwinist vision arguably reflects a conception of how markets operate that owes more to economic theory than any observation of reality. It is open to question how far these idealised representations of unbounded competition offer an accurate analysis of the complex relationships and functions of markets, or provide a feasible blueprint for the real-life behaviour of organisations. Chambers (1988: 47) emphasises that 'policy debates can be conducted without having to refer to the quirks of actual markets', and that there exist hundreds of different types of market.

At the same time, debate about the efficacy of market mechanisms has thrown up a number of problems with the operation of markets. These range from outright market failure when attempting to deal in the supply of 'public goods' such as training (see Olson, 1971; Streeck, 1989), through problems of ensuring the adequate supply and transmission of information to actors within a market, to lags in the response time of markets to new levels and patterns of demand. Many of these issues have implications for the operation of the market in education which the government has sought to create.

Limits to competition

Perhaps most importantly, if we examine how businesses relate to the environmental context of operating in real-life markets, we see that purist models do not always hold good. Experience tends to suggest that total competition is rare, and that, within many markets, companies act to place limits on competition, through a wide variety of means.

Why should this be the case? Numerous writers have argued that organisations operating within an uncertain environment will seek to establish a situation whereby risk is minimised (Gospel, 1973; Simon, 1959; Cyert & March, 1963). Firms recognise that the total, unregulated competition of the economists' theoretical marketplace creates levels of complexity and instability which make management impossible. Companies, often acting collectively, will therefore try to limit uncertainty.

In attempting to do this, firms may develop interdependent relationships with other elements and groups within the environment (Gospel, 1973: 219). Through such relationships, a set of implicit or explicit behavioural norms or conventions will evolve which act to restrict fluctuations in the intentions and actions of actors within the firm's environment. These interdependent relationships can take a variety of institutional forms, including cartels (which may be legal or illegal), technical agreements, licencing agreements, franchise and agency agreements, the developement of shareholdings in customers and/or suppliers, and other forms of vertical integration (Richardson, 1972: 895). Another variation is the establishment of standardised codes of 'good business practice' within an industry or product market, and the use of trade and employer associations in channelling and regulating interdependence (Cyert & March, 1963: 120). Indeed, many employer associations were created to help stop predatory price competition between firms (Clegg, 1964).

Market control

To focus on just one way in which companies may attempt to place limits on competition, firms may use collective bargaining, particularly at national level, to reduce or avoid risk and uncertainty through the imposition and maintenance of market control. Market control is exercised by the removal of wages, or more accurately labour costs, from competition, through negotiation of a common minimum level of pay and conditions across the whole of the industry. Undercutting because of low labour costs is thereby avoided (Flanders, 1974: 355).

Historically, attempts to achieve market control underpinned the development of employer organisations in the UK. In highly competitive industries, such as construction, printing, clothing, garages, road haulage, baking, and electrical contracting, which are all characterised by small employers (small especially in relation to the unions that face them); intense product market competition in local or national markets; capital costs which are low in comparison with labour costs; and by low profit margins, there are overall advantages to employers in avoiding the uncertainty and instability generated by unrestricted competition.

Moreover, these concerns are heightened by the fact that undercutting, in sectors such as construction and the garage trade, is often associated with 'cowboy' firms whose standards of service to the customer are of such a low level as to bring the whole industry into disrepute. Quite often, extensive efforts are made by employer associations to regulate the conduct of their members, in terms of both adherence to national wage rates and standards of service to customers. One example is the electrical contracting industry, where employers who attempt to offer pay and conditions in excess of those laid down in the national agreement face expulsion from the employers' organisation.

The lessons for a market in education

The measures described above, to which companies resort in order to limit the uncertainty created by market competition, have a number of implications for attempts to introduce market mechanisms within the education system. The first message that emerges from the attempts of some business sectors to achieve market control through national collective bargaining, is that in an education system where schools are in competition with one another, the rationale for some form of national bargaining over pay and conditions of service may actually be strengthened.

A second, and somewhat broader message, is that the problems of achieving unrestrained market competition in the private sector beg the question of how realistic it is to expect such behaviour to be adopted by schools. Certainly some schools have enthusiastically embarked on radical new programmes to attract additional pupils, with major marketing initiatives and even offers of free gifts to new parents (Lodge, 1989). On the whole, however, schools have appeared reluctant to embrace this type of philosophy, and the result has been a number of widely reported attempts by groups of schools to avoid direct competition with one another by establishing various forms of co-operative arrangements. These have included attempts to establish local marketing consortia and joint marketing schemes (Nash, 1989; Makins, 1990). In addition, the National Association of Head Teachers (NAHT) has been working to design a code of conduct that will define the limits of acceptable competitive behaviour between state schools (Blackburn, 1990).

These attempts should not be viewed as being somehow symptomatic of a public sector refusal to behave like businesses. Indeed, quite the reverse. The desire to find mechanisms that will place limits on disruptive and destructive competitive behaviour, and which emphasise collective solutions to relating to the marketplace and the pressure it generates, are an example of public sector managers adopting forms of action that closely mirror those found in the private sector.

In any event, it seems important that if markets are seen as the answer to problems in the public sector, and the behaviour of private sector business organisations operating within market discipline as the new model for the management and control of public services, policy makers' understanding of how markets function and how companies operate within them needs to accord with reality. If this is not the case, then there is a danger that schools may find themselves being asked to copy an idealised and abstracted model of behaviour that is rarely actually exhibited by private sector companies.

The Complexity of Private Sector Managerial Behaviour

If models of economic activity predicated on unlimited competition are perhaps over-simplified, what of the models of private sector managerial activity which educationalists are being exhorted to consider adopting? To begin with, there is a problem with the way in which much of the prescriptive management literature chooses to promote an idealised model of management activity which often bears little resemblance to what happens, even in large, apparently sophisticated organisations.

The gap between theory and practice

To take a single strand of managerial activity — that of personnel management — it is apparent that a considerable gap exists between the mass of prescriptive literature and reality. As Sisson (1990: 4) points out:

> While there is no shortage of texts telling managers what to do, there has been little description, let alone analysis, of what happens in practice. Crucially, there is usually very little discussion of the appropriateness of the techniques or, indeed, of the problems managers experience in applying them; the reader has to take on trust the prescriptions offered. (Sisson, 1990: 4)

Recent research indicates that the development of coherent company personnel policies and their integration within companies' broader business strategies (Marginson *et al.*, 1988; Purcell, 1989), manpower or human resource planning (Timperley & Sisson, 1989), recruitment and selection (Collinson, 1988), and training and development (Keep, 1989), all provide examples of sharp divergence between the ideal model and everyday reality in UK businesses.

The issue for those in education, is whether they are being expected to emulate the often confused and less than perfect reality that pertains in many private sector organisations, or to attempt to copy an idealised model of managerial activity that encompasses levels of performance achieved in Britain by only a very limited number of atypical, often foreign-owned private sector organisations.

One of the potential benefits for schools of learning from industry, is the opportunity to profit from the mistakes and problems highlighted by companies' attempts to introduce new styles and methods of management. By learning from others' experiences the drawbacks and pitfalls, and by discovering how best to avoid them, schools can ease the learning curve through which they will pass in adopting new methods of management. This can only happen, however, if private sector management practice is presented to educationalists through critical analysis, which acknowledges the problems and failures as well as the successes.

A variety of models

A further point worth making is that private sector management practice is not unitary. There is no single private sector model of management that schools can adopt, for a great variety of management control structures and styles are to be found in companies operating in the UK.

The importance of this observation needs to be underlined. If we examine personnel management, it is clear that there is no single private sector model. Indeed, a wide variety of styles of personnel management and industrial relations have been identified (Sisson, 1989a). Thus, even where there is a common thread to some elements of management's objectives, for example a desire to avoid unionisation, the means to the end, in terms of management style and actions, may vary very considerably. Both Marks & Spencer, and Grunwicks, sought to avoid the unionisation of their workplaces. The means by which this common objective was pursued by these two organisations could hardly have been more different.

Besides this variety of styles or approaches to personnel management, there is much evidence that even the definition of what constitutes personnel management has shifted over time. It may also be observed that there is considerable debate, both among personnel practitioners and academics, concerning the relative merits of the different conceptions of personnel management currently on offer, particularly in relation to whether traditional personnel management is being replaced by a new, more strategically-oriented human resource management (HRM), and if it is being so replaced, whether this is a desirable development (see Sisson, 1989b; Storey, 1989).

Diversity in management structures

The range of managerial styles and approaches to personnel issues found within UK industry is broadly representative of the diversity of managerial practice across a whole range of corporate activities. Perhaps most importantly, the ways in which companies design and operate their strategic control and internal mangement structures vary considerably, and differences in the configuration of these materially affect the style and scope of a whole range of subsiduary, or second and third order managerial activities, such as personnel management (Goold & Campbell, 1986; Purcell, 1989).

It is to these fundamentally important strategic and structural arrangements that we now turn. What follows is a very brief outline of some of the basic models of business organisation — the small business, critical function, and multi-divisional (M-form). It should be emphasised that these are simplified models, and that in practice many UK firms have hybrid management structures that are being subject to rapid change. Nevertheless, as we shall see, these basic models offer divergent blueprints for the organisation and control of education.

The small, autonomous business is the simplest form. Within the small firm, operations usually cover only a few sites or units, and the development of specialised managerial functions will be limited. Lacking the problem of co-ordinating the activities of multiple operating units, internal control systems will be simple.

Critical function organisations are those running a number of businesses or outlets, which are usually operating in either a single area or closely related areas of business activity. They maintain strong corporate headquarters that formulated strategic policies, covering areas such as product mix, pricing, investment decisions, and personnel policies. A divisional structure may also exist. Operational responsibility for implementation of centrally determined policies rests with the manager of the individual operating unit. A good example of critical function organisation would be a clearing bank, or a supermarket chain. See Figure 9.1.

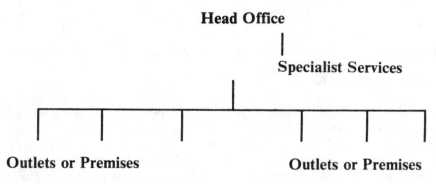

Head Office

Specialist Services

Outlets or Premises　　　　　　**Outlets or Premises**

FIGURE 9.1 *Critical function model*

Multi-divisional or M-form has evolved as the classic structural arrangement for managing large, diversified businesses. The organisation has three tiers — company headquarters, divisions (usually each with its own divisional HQ), and individual subsiduaries (see Figure 9.2). Responsibility for some strategic decisions may rest with the company headquarters alone, while others are shared with or are totally the responsibility of the division.

A development of M-form that has recently become popular is the move towards greater emphasis upon the *strategic business unit (SBU)* (see Figure 9.3). In companies that have gone down this route, the corporate headquarters has a 'hands off' policy, its role being largely limited to setting and monitoring in detail the financial performance of the individual businesses, and in acting as investment banker to them. The role of divisions has been weakened, or abolished, and responsibility pushed down to the individual subsidiary. Within the tight, often short-term focused financial controls exerted by the centre, the manager of the individual stratetic business unit is expected to exercise considerable discretion over its operation. GEC is a good example of a company that has adopted the concept of strategic business units.

Associated with these different structures is a fundamental choice about

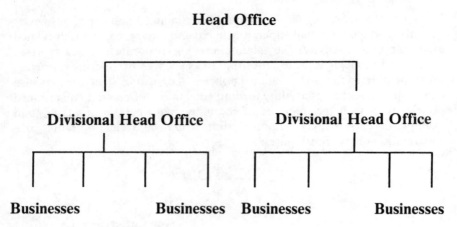

FIGURE 9.2 *M-form model*

how the business is to be controlled internally. Put crudely, there are three basic models. Firstly, the *strategic planner*, where the company headquarters exist to 'lead a wide search for the best strategic options, and tenaciously pursues ambitious long-term goals' (Goold & Campbell, 1986: 10). Examples would be companies like BP and United Biscuits. Secondly, and in direct contrast, there are the *financial controllers*, who are more concerned with short-term planning and results, and who 'peer at the business through numbers' (Goold & Campbell, 1986: 118). Examples here would be Hanson Trust, GEC, and Tarmac. Finally, there are the *strategic control* companies, who attempt to find a middle way between the extremes of the above two models. Companies that fall into this category would include Courtaulds, ICI, and Vickers.

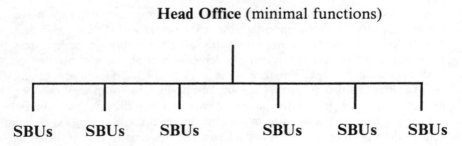

FIGURE 9.3 *SBU model*

The implications of managerial diversity

This diversity of private sector managerial style and practice has a number of implications for current education reforms. The first, and most obvious, is that there is no single, simple model there to be copied or adapted by managers within the education system. What exists is a vast and potentially confusing range of approaches to managerial problems. It is easy to suggest that, in general terms, schools need to learn from private sector management and run themselves on more businesslike lines; the problem is knowing what this might actually mean in terms of selecting appropriate models for change from a broad spectrum of practices.

These problems partly reflect the fact that current policies towards schools show limited appreciation of the issue of management structures. It is hard to detect any real recognition that in the private sector there are the competing and fundamentally different models of management structure outlined above. Traditionally, the school education system has unconsciously mirrored the multi-divisional model, with the Department of Education and Science (DES) as company HQ, the Local Education Authority (LEA) as the division structure that managed the individual school. The Education Reform Act (ERA) changed this structure, and it is currently by no means apparent whether it is the individual school, or the school system as a whole, that is being seen as a business. There is also a lack of clarity about exactly where within education the very different responsibilities for strategic and operational management should rest. Arguably, three quite different models of private sector managerial structure are simultaneously being embraced by educational policy makers.

Firstly, there is the 'critical function' model. If this is applied to education, the state school system is treated as a single business, with the DES assuming the role of corporate headquarters, the LEA either becomes the divisional or disappears, and the school becomes the individual outlet. The DES controls the overall product mix (curriculum), and develops stronger functional responsibilities for the strategic management of issues such as personnel policy. The LEA (if it still exists) provides a limited range of specialised services, and the school is responsible for operationalising DES policies.

Secondly, there is the SBU model. In the context of the education system, its adoption would see a major strategic role of the DES in establishing performance targets, setting spending levels, and monitoring and inspecting performance. There would be a strong emphasis on short-term planning horizons and cost-minimisation. Divisional management, in the shape of the

LEA, would wither away and the centre would devolve responsibility for many issues, such as the curriculum mix, and pay and personnel policies, to the individual school.

The final basic model, is that of the free-standing small business. A good example of this model being applied to education is given by Stuart Sexton, an ex-advisor to Sir Keith Joseph, and now director of the education unit at the Institute of Economic Affairs. Sexton (1990) sees education policies as ultimately leading towards a situation where each school is an independent small business. There will no longer be any state schools as such — all will be independent and private. Funding will be vouchers-based, with parents free to top-up their value. There will be no central control over and above the annual decision by the Treasury concerning the level of the voucher. Both the DES and LEAs will vanish, as there will be no role left for them. Current policies, Sexton argues, are a halfway-house between the centralised, bureaucratic model of the past; and the free market in education which he envisages.

The fact that current policies appear to unconsciously embrace random and ultimately conflicting elements of all three of these models makes for confusion. Thus the national curriculum represents a centralised 'critical function' style control of the product mix, while at the same time, individual schools (or outlets) are expected to operate, not as parts of a rationalised chain, but as atomised small businesses in competition with one another.

Not only is there a lack of clarity about what lessons the education system is supposed to be learning from business, and from whom in business it is meant to be learning them, but there is also a degree of inherent confusion about who in education is meant to be doing the learning. An example here, is the question of who is to be held accountable for what. Uncertainty about whether the school is meant to be an independent small business, or acting as a business unit within State School Education plc, makes for muddled lines of accountability. Whereas great stress has been laid upon the need for schools and LEAs to be responsive and accountable to their customers, comparatively little has been heard about the accountability of 'corporate headquarters' — the DES. If schools are to be measured by performance indicators, there is an argument for suggesting that similar instruments be applied to the quality of the strategic management of the school system being supplied by the DES (Brighouse, 1988b). Perhaps most importantly, as Newsam (1989) has suggested, in a situation where 'the education system and its resources are controlled from the centre and curriculum requirements with statutory force need resources', responsibility for the effects of strategic decisions about the level of resourcing ought to rest at the centre.

Confusion about the allocation of responsibility within the system, brings us to perhaps the most important constraint on the education system's choice of managerial borrowings from the private sector. This relates to the problem of management systems as structures shaped and governed by certain fundamental strategic goals. If most managerial activity is contingent upon choices about the fundamental strategy of the organisation; in particular its choice between the different types of managerial control structures outlined above, and the ways that it confronts the opportunities afforded by the product markets in which it operates, then attempts to copy isolated second and third order elements of managerial systems without reference to the strategic setting in which they operate, may have unintended consequences or prove fruitless.

To put it in a slightly different way, managerial systems operate as a totality. Hence individual aspects or components of the corporate managerial process interrelate and interact to produce the overall effectiveness or otherwise of the system. Managerial styles and techniques adopted to deal with particular issues tend to flow from the overall strategic aims and objectives of the organisation. For instance, attitudes towards product or service quality have implications for the design of work, for training, and for reward structures within the organisation. As a result, attempts to abstract single elements from the system, without reference to the synergistic relationships that exist between them, will potentially produce sub-optimal results. Choice of management style, if it is to prove effective in the long term, may therefore not be amenable to a 'pick 'n mix' approach.

Thus, managerial styles and methods have to be appropriate to the task in hand. The management processes that have been designed to run a fast food chain will not necessarily be applicable in managing a computer company, and what might work in either of these companies may not be what is required to order the activities of an inner-city comprehensive. Management systems designed around the primary task of cost-minimisation and the enhancement of short-term profit are arguably not those best suited to the long-term development of an effective school. As Everard (1986: 190–1), in his influential book on developing management in schools, cautions, 'education needs to discriminate between different managerial approaches and adopt only those that speak to the condition of education'.

Finally, there is the risk that, if the education system and schools are not presented with a critical and up-to-date analysis of managerial techniques, they will find themselves adopting practices whose effectiveness is now being called into doubt. One danger in the wake of the introduction of LMS, is that schools and LEAs will adopt 'financial controller' style systems of management. Yet research indicates that these decentralised models of management and accounting, budgeting and cost control systems may be suitable only for businesses dealing in simple products (Prahalad & Hamel, 1990). Numerous commentators and managers (see, for example, Armstrong, 1989; Johnson & Kaplan, 1987; Allen, 1985) have questioned the wisdom of traditional cost accounting systems, pointing to the dangers inherent in concentrating power within managerial control structures geared towards short-term cost minimisation, and to the damaging long-term effects of numbers-driven rather than issue-driven management (McKinsey & Co, 1988: 49). Given the complexity of the educational product, and the long lead times involved, a broad 'strategic planner' approach to the management of the education service would appear the most appropriate road to take.

The Differences Between Schools and Businesses

Discussion has so far concentrated on the variety, and complexity of operation, of market systems and management structures that schools could adopt. There remains the fundamental question of how far schools, and the state school system as a whole, reproduce the conditions within which private sector activity takes place. Is it possible to run schools like businesses?

Building on the basic model of public and private management domains developed by Stewart & Ranson (1988), the section that follows briefly examines how far state schools replicate the conditions of private sector businesses, and hence the degree to which they can be run as such. Stewart & Ranson suggest that management in the 'public domain' is fundamentally distinct from private sector management, in terms of objectives, modes of operation, and constraints upon performance. There are, moreover, 'many aspects of management in the public domain that find no ready parallel in the private sector' (Stewart & Ranson, 1988: 13).

It can certainly be argued that there are a group of quite profound structural differences that differentiate schools from businesses. To begin with, schools do not charge a price upon which they aim to make a profit, but instead have a public service obligation to provide a free service to all those who are legally entitled. There is also the expectation that schools are there to pursue social goals, such as the moral and religious development of the pupil and the fostering of notions of citizenship, which are not normally expected of private sector organisations.

Because of the lack of a direct price mechanism, schools also find it less easy to identify their 'customers'. In one sense, every adult citizen as a tax or community charge payer is a consumer because they are paying for the education service. The government appears to view parents as the main customer, but it has also identified employers as an important consumer group. From the school's perspective, the pupils are likely to be seen as the direct consumer of the services being offered (Horn, 1987). It should be noted that the interests of these various 'customers' will not always coincide. For instance, parents' and pupils' views of what constitute the best subject specialisms and career choices to pursue, may not match what employers want.

At the same time, the market which individual state schools operate in is more rigorously regulated than most private sector business markets, and is state rather than self-regulated. The government establish, in detail, the basis upon which, and the rules by which, competition will take place. They also specify the information that must be disclosed to customers, and control the product range being offered. Interestingly, given the emphasis placed upon the value of the 'level playing field' of competition, these controls do not apply to private schools. Thus, while it may be true that state schools now operate in what can broadly be termed a market, there are various ways in which this market is currently structured and regulated differently from that faced by most private sector business organisations.

Perhaps the most fundamental difference is that the management of public sector organisations is part of, and subject to, the political process in a way in which private businesses are not. As Ferner (1988) demonstrates, this is true even of nationalised industries. For public sector services such as education and health, the impact of political considerations is likely to be even greater. In such circumstances, strategic choices about issues such as levels of service and product mix, will not be the result of market forces, but will instead express 'values determined through the political process in response to a changing environment' (Stewart & Ranson, 1988: 13).

One example would be the national curriculum (Sexton, 1990). Consumers were not asked their preferences through market surveys. This new 'product' was not tested through trial launches in a limited number of outlets in order to gauge consumer reaction. Nor have market mechanisms enabled parents to choose the subjects included in the curriculum, or determine the balance of emphasis between these subjects. In fact, the national curriculum is the result not of market forces, but of political decisions by the Secretary of State for Education, his civil servants and advisers. Another example would be the trade-off within the school system between opting out and open enrolment on one hand, and the efficient use of limited public resources on the other. As Quentin Thompson (1990), one of the authors of the Coopers & Lybrand report on LMS points out, this 'can only be a political decision'.

Furthermore, if we examine just one specific dimension of managerial activity — revenue generation and budgetary control, it is clear that there are significant differences between a school and a business. As has been pointed out above, state schools lack a direct price mechanism and must provide a 'free' service to consumers. Goods and services are not sold, instead taxes (whether local or national) are raised to pay for the activity, and, as a result, schools cannot price up to what the market will stand. Because income from consumers cannot be raised with respect to a state school's primary product — the education of pupils — income generation to supplement central and local government funding can take place only within a relatively narrow range of secondary or peripheral activities. In essence, state schools may engage in varying forms of fund-raising, they do not exist to trade as businesses.

At the same time, individual state schools have, compared to a small business, limited discretion over a number of financial operating conditions. The national curriculum means that their ability to alter the product mix, and drop lines (subjects) that are expensive to provide, such as science, is heavily circumscribed. They cannot choose to alter their customer base, move up market, and refuse to provide a service to those who cause the school to incur disproportionate costs, such as disruptive pupils, or children of below average ability (unless the school is operating within a selective system). Nor can state schools realise their capital assets, operate deficit budgeting, or, in normal circumstances, borrow capital against future income.

In general terms, a number of differences separate the shape, complexity and detail of the managerial task in a state school from that in a private sector business enterprise. These disimilarities are each important, and when taken together represent a fundamental divergence in the nature and basis of management decision making. Stewart & Ranson's distinctions between the public and private domains serve to remind us that, whatever the rhetoric, and whatever the similarities between some aspects of school and business activity, the state school is not a business. Its aims and objectives, and the rules under which it operates, are different, and it is the political process, rather than the profit motive, that ultimately determines the scale and nature of its operation.

The existence of these dissimilarities underscores the need for caution in the utilisation of private sector management models in the state school system. In particular, there are dangers in simply trying to read across from private sector business practice, and in prescribing it as a model that be directly applied in solving the entire range of challenges which state schools face in the 1990s. If schools are to learn from the private sector, the sorts of differences outlined above need to be borne in mind, and to inform the choice and method of application of private sector structures and practices. Failure to appreciate those areas where the two sectors differ, and to respect the often fundamental nature of these divergences, is likely to lead to managerial transplants that will be unsuccessful and short-lived. The blanket application of contextually inappropriate styles of management, whether by school heads and governors, LEA officers, civil servants, consultants, or politicians, will in all probability be doomed to end in failure.

Some Final Thoughts

There is one final point that needs to be addressed. It might be suggested that this paper has been based upon a misapprehension, and that at least some commentators and politicians are not expecting schools to copy specific aspects of business practice, but simply in a general sense to learn from, or be inspired by, business's efficiency and cost effectiveness. The difficulty with this line of argument, is that it has little to say about what the process of learning from or being inspired by business might mean in practice for schools or managers within the education system.

Leaving aside the question of whether cost effectiveness, efficiency, and an ability to manage change are in fact common characteristics in the average UK private enterprise; where these characteristics exist, they do not arise of themselves. They may constitute desired ends, but they are achieved only as a result of specific management structures, techniques and procedures. If schools are to emulate the believed success of private sector businesses, as defined in terms of cost effectiveness and efficiency, then it seems likely that there will be attempts to transfer the mechanisms and forms of behaviour that create and support that effectivness. Moreover, numerous mechanisms of transference exist, in the shape of staff secondment schemes, do-it-yourself management textbooks, and various forms of consultancy.

It is precisely because specific structures and techniques produce certain sorts of results, and mould the organisations that use them in certain sorts of ways, that this paper argues that great care needs to be exercised over the choice and adoption of such structures and techniques. As Everard (1986: 190) points out, 'there are enough examples of incompetent or inappropriate industrial management practices, and enough public criticism of the performance of British industry, to make it prudent to be circumspect in tranplanting to schools management practices from industry'. This is not say that it should not be attempted, but that such attempts need to be carefully thought through, and to take account of some of the issues raised above.

Acknowledgements

The author would like to record his thanks to colleagues in the Industrial Relations Research Unit of Warwick University, in particular Professor Keith Sisson, Paul Edwards, and Anthony Ferner, for their helpful comments and suggestions concerning this paper. As ever, any errors, omissions, or weaknesses of argument remain the sole responsibility of the author. The work of the IRRU is funded by the Economic and Social Research Council.

10 School Development Plans: Their History and Their Potential

MARILYN LEASK

Introduction

This chapter traces the growth of planning of in-service training (INSET) and whole school development in England and Wales, and explores the potential role of the school development plan (SDP) in the locally managed schools of the 1990s.

The development of the whole school planning process is placed within the context of the political influences on education over the last decade. The loss of autonomy of schools, the move to central government control and the attempts to increase local accountability through the governing body have had profound implications for the ways schools are managed. Attention is drawn to the advantages of a whole school approach to planning (resulting in the production, implementation and evaluation of a school development plan) in enabling heads and governing bodies to manage the changes they are currently facing and will continue to face into the 1990s.

The Challenge of the 1990s

How can standards be raised? This question was centre-stage in the educational debates of the 1980s. Resulting legislation (the 1986 and 1988 Education Acts) has meant that much of previous practice in education both in management and curriculum terms, has been uprooted and even that which was flourishing has been in danger of being swept away. Schools are entering the 1990s grappling with major change on two fronts: curriculum and management.

Curriculum. The progressive implementation of a national curriculum and its accompanying assessment procedures will continue to require a significant proportion of the school's resources, both in materials and staff time. Modification and adjustment on the basis of experience will be a feature of work in schools to the end of the century.

Management. In a number of fundamental ways, the locally managed schools of the 1990s will function differently to those of the early 1980s. Heads and governors are now in the position of managing the school collaboratively. This is not to say that their roles are the same, but that the balance of power has changed and governors have a much more demanding role than before the 1986 Act. Heads and governors are required to become:

- more accountable to parents (schemes of work have to be available for parents to view; results of national curriculum assessments are to be published)
- responsive to the community (through increased community representation on the governing body; through open enrolment)
- responsible for matters previously the domain of the LEA (aspects of finance, staffing matters, internal maintenance of premises).

The school — LEA relationship is also changing rapidly. LEAs have a duty to ensure that the national curriculum is implemented and many have restructured their service, often limiting or abolishing the traditional advisory roles in favour of inspection (Audit Commission, 1989a, 1989b).

At the same time, the very existence of LEAs is being questioned and the idea that all schools should be grant maintained and centrally funded is being put forward.

Faced with such increased accountability, changed responsibilities and greater community involvement, the head and governing body need to develop new strategies for managing the school *together*. The change to local management of schools (LMS) is often misinterpreted as being principally about financial issues. Concerns over inadequate funding have led to this focusing of attention on finance but LMS involves far more fundamental change than acquiring the ability to balance the school budget. As the Coopers & Lybrand (1988: 5) report to the DES points out: 'The changes [to LMS] require a new culture and philosophy of the organisation of education at the school level. They are more than purely financial; they need a general shift in management.' The contribution which the school development planning process and the plan itself can make to the management of schools facing these challenges is explored later in the paper. Initially, the background prompting the production of formal INSET and school development plans

(SDPs) is documented and the evolutionary path of SDPs is charted. The final section of the paper looks at the dilemmas schools and governing bodies face in managing their schools effectively in the 1990s and the role of the SDP in supporting this work.

The 1980s: Schools Lose Their Autonomy

Over the decade, the traditional autonomy of schools was whittled away to be replaced by centralised control over the curriculum and INSET, and increased accountability to the local community directly (rather than through the LEA). Three major influences on schools during this time provided foundations for the development of formal whole school planning approaches.

Firstly, the introduction of the Technical Vocational Education Initiative (TVEI) in the secondary and FE sector in 1982 meant that LEAs were required to submit bids to the Manpower Services Commission for resources and approval of schemes. Many saw this as an attempt by central government to manipulate the curriculum by direct control of the purse strings. Previously a school's funds were provided through the LEA with decisions about the curriculum being taken within the school. However, whatever the intention, one effect was to develop planning skills among those involved.

Secondly, central funds were made available for INSET through TRIST (TVEI-related in-service training), then GRIST (grant-related in-service training, which then included the primary sector), then LEATGS (LEA training grants scheme). Again, LEAs had to bid for funds. The aim was to ensure the provision of INSET in areas targeted by central government. There was also some funding for local priorities. In the summer of 1990 LEATGS gave way to GEST (grants for educational support and training) which combined both LEATGS and EGS (Education Support Grant) programmes. Funding for local priorities was dropped. This hit LEAs, schools and teachers hard: often this money was delegated directly to schools or used to provide teachers' centres and advisory teacher support.

Accompanying the requirement to bid for resources in these areas, was the demand that the use of resources be based on identified needs and that such provision be evaluated. To do this effectively, LEAs and schools developed strategies for identifying needs and evaluating subsequent provision. Many LEAs required the schools to produce 'INSET plans' and 'TVEI plans'. These new practices provided sound foundations for whole school planning.

Thirdly, 'Baker Days' or 'professional training days' (1986 onwards) provided the time and the opportunity for teachers to discuss professional matters at length. As school development planning requires whole staff involvement, its widespread adoption would have been much more difficult if such opportunities for discussion had not existed.

Throughout this period, the Government believed it had a mandate to bring about radical and rapid change on a national scale and legislation in the form of the 1986 and 1988 Acts was a predictable outcome. Both these Acts fundamentally challenge the traditional roles of heads and the governing body — demanding at the very least, an approach to school management based on partnership with the community through governors. In preparing the ground for LMS, Coopers & Lybrand highlight the need for the head and governing body work together:

> LMS will succeed only if there is a positive attitude to it from the head, the staff and the governing body. It will require a recognition that it is school management that is needed not simply an increase in administration. (Coopers & Lybrand, 1988: 6)

Some hold the view that governing bodies were intended to be the more powerful partner: '. . . the newly constituted governing bodies would be about the consumers of education: parents and employers who would lick the teachers and local authorities into shape' (Hemmings, 1990: 16). In either case, new ways of working for heads and governors are clearly required under LMS. Yet the evidence is that for many heads and governing bodies, communities and schools, such ways of working are as yet to be devised (Hemmings, Deem & Brehany, 1990).

There is widespread uncertainty about how the new partnership is to work. This is hardly surprising given that governing bodies are obliged to meet only once a term and thus may still have had very few meetings since the 1988 Act was passed. The research of Rosemary Deem and Kevin Brehony on the ESRC funded project 'The reform of school governing bodies', notes the concerns felt by governors: 'A big worry for all the governing bodies in our study has been how they can discharge all their responsibilities while still continuing to do their jobs, eat, sleep and see their families' (Deem & Brehony, 1990: 20).

Schools involved in the SDP project reported that school development planning provides a useful way of developing this partnership. Of course, the notion of planning a school's development is not new. Heads have always planned and had a vision for their school. It is the change to LMS which requires this vision to be shared and developed openly with governors and parents. Some schools extend this involvement to pupils.

School Development Plans: Evolution and Growth

Formal SDPs were in existence well before LMS made such planning desirable. Both Goddard (1985) and the Thomas Report (ILEA, 1985) mention the value to schools of such a plan.

Goddard, in addressing the issues raised by the then recently published recommendations of the Advisory Committee for the Supply and Education of Teachers (ACSET) on in-service training, focuses on the need to plan provision of INSET. He describes a school development plan as providing 'an enabling mechanism' which allows institutions and LEAs to move beyond the stage of simply making statements about ideal provision to a stage which involves charting 'the route, timetable, the necessary linkage and the means by which agreement is achieved' (Goddard, 1985: 243).

The Thomas Report, which was concerned with improving the quality of primary education in Inner London, described the SDP as having a '. . . central purpose . . . expressed in terms of the improvements sought in the children's learning . . . [It is] a contract between the head and the staff to which, in the end, all must subscribe (ILEA, 1985: 77). At the same time, another LEA (Enfield) advised schools, in the light of the national debate on the curriculum, to:

- establish curriculum aims and set objectives and goals as means of achieving these aims
- devise a development and institutional plan to achieve these aims and to handle and manage change in the future
- develop an appropriate staff development framework, policy and programme to enable staff to have the confidence and expertise to handle and manage change in the future.
(London Borough of Enfield, 1985: 1)

Such whole school planning required simple and manageable procedures for identifying priorities on which to work and approaches to school self-evaluation or whole school review which were developed through the 1980s provided firm foundations on which to base a school development plan. The availability of strategies such as Guidelines for Review and Internal Development in Schools (GRIDS, an SCDC (Schools Curriculum Development Committee) project), IMTEC (International Movement Towards Educational Change), as well as the school self-evaluation schemes produced by many LEAs (notably ILEA and Oxfordshire), enabled schools to improve the quality and depth of their internal reviews and development.

In its advice for secondary schools, ILEA recommended that the development plan be linked to such a review process:

Central to such a review will be a development plan for the school which combines accurate analysis of work and developments to date with a clear statement of priorities for the future. The development plan must be related to all aspects of the school, the quality of work in the classroom, the organisation of the school, the planning of curriculum development and the process of reviewing and responding to staff development needs. (ILEA, 1988: 2)

In many LEAs the SDP was, for a few years seen as an INSET plan, as the introduction of targeted funding for INSET (through TRIST/GRIST/LEATGS) was the driving force behind the introduction of development planning. Secondary schools often had TVEI plans but these were separate from other aspects of school planning — perhaps partly because they were required to be presented in a particular way at a particular time, to a particular external audience. Integration of different aspects of planning to produce a coherent whole school plan was not automatic and the research undertaken on the SDP project revealed that this lack of integration was problematic for schools.

In some LEAs, little if anything was done to develop school self-review or INSET planning. Schools in such LEAs were at a disadvantage when, in the late 1980s the introduction of the national curriculum and the move to full financial control required those managing the school to have well-developed planning and management skills. At this point, the proliferation of a variety of terms which described aspects of whole school planning caused considerable confusion. Heads and governors were advised to draw up management plans (DES, 1988a: sections 21 and 22) as well as national curriculum development plans (DES letter to CEOs, 17th February 1989, from Jenny Bacon). Even those schools with considerable experience in systematically planning whole school development were protesting that they appeared to be expected to have several sets of plans to satisfy different demands.

Recognising the need for a nationally coherent approach, the DES funded the SDP project in April 1989. This project aimed to identify good practice and provide advice to LEAs, schools and governing bodies on school development planning and advice was provided for both LEAs and schools over the period 1989 to 1990 (Hargreaves, Hopkins & Leask, 1989a; 1989b; 1990; Hargreaves & Hopkins, 1991). As yet it is too early to evaluate the impact of this advice, particularly as the changes brought about by the 1988 Act mean that even those schools experienced in development planning had to change certain aspects of their practice in order to manage the new financial and staffing responsibilities, involve the governing body more fully, take account of the changed LEA role, allow for the impact on parents of increased 'parent power' and plan curriculum changes including cross-curricular work.

Two concurrent initiatives have also produced advice on school management issues: The LMS Initiative (in 1989) and the School Management Task Force (in 1991).

In these various ways, the purpose of school development planning has evolved beyond simply developing the curriculum coherently in the light of the aims of the school and planning appropriate INSET to linking curriculum development with the allocation of resources and communicating the direction of the school to a much wider audience. However the central purpose remains unchanged. It is to enable the school as a whole to develop its work within a planned and coherent framework so that the quality of the educational provision for the children improves.

School Development Plans and School Management in the 1990s

'Talk about children's education on governing bodies is relatively rare yet clearly this may not be because there is no desire to do so' (Deem & Brehony, 1990: 20). This statement encapsulates a central dilemma faced by heads and governing bodies in moving to a more collaborative relationship. A key assumption underpinning the reforms is that governors have or can acquire fairly quickly through training, the knowledge and experience required to allow them to take on their new responsibilities. Yet for many governors the curriculum is uncharted territory. Their knowledge often limited to their own experience at school and that of their children. By contrast, teachers base their decisions on the knowledge of the achievements of the hundreds and thousands of children who pass through their care.

From the research carried out on the SDPs project it was apparent that collaborative work on planning provided conditions for the growth of an informed dialogue between governors, head and staff. At each stage of the planning process, decisions are made based on professional judgements and it is in sharing this decision making with staff that governors can develop their own professional judgement in the educational context. Hemmings, Deem & Brehony (1990) provide evidence for the urgent need for governors to improve their knowledge of educational issues. The report of the DES/HMI conference on governing bodies (DES/HMI, 1991) provides guidelines for governors and heads about developing appropriate relationships.

To sum up, four particular ways in which the development planning process seems to support the work of headteachers and governing bodies are:

– in linking curriculum development, staff development and INSET with the allocation of resources

- in promoting effective ways of working for the head and governing body
- in enhancing communication with parents
- in providing a basis for discussion with LEAs and HMI.

Curriculum development, staff development, INSET and resource allocation

'Spending decisions are best made by those most closely involved with a school — the governors and headteacher' (DES, 1987b: 10). Unfortunately the premise that governors are so closely involved with the school is shaky. Pupils, teachers and support staff and parents are more knowledgeable than the majority of governors by virtue of their daily contact with the school. Ensuring that planning is influenced primarily by curriculum needs is crucial to efficient development of the main work of the school which is after all, the delivery of the curriculum so that children learn. Yet those with a thorough knowledge of curriculum issues are probably a small minority on most governing bodies. There is an urgent need for governors to become knowledgeable about the curriculum if they are to make sound decisions about the deployment of the school's budget.

Deem & Brehony (1990: 20) identify an additional problem over governors' control of the budget: 'If care is not taken, their [governors'] concern with children and young people's education will vanish in the desire to manage budgets. Can this really be what the proponents of the Reform Act wanted?' They also note that the engagement of governors with issues does seem to depend on their knowledge and experience:

> The extent of governors' contributions seems to depend a good deal on the issue under discussion. Thus co-opted governors are particularly vocal on finance issues (where schools are sometimes compared unfavourably to businesses); vicars and those with strong religious affiliations are liable to get excited about collective worship and parents are often concerned about teacher supply problems and safety issues. (Deem & Brehony, 1990: 20)

There is evidence too that in some cases governing bodies may direct finance into areas with which they are familiar (e.g. premises) at the expense of the curriculum. How will governors decide on how to prioritise spending on INSET and staff development? Altruism has been a feature of much staff development up till now. INSET and staff development programmes have often enabled those undertaking them to move to senior positions in different schools and LEAs other than those which sponsored their training. Will governors feel they have an obligation to develop the expertise in the profession as a whole?

Some governing bodies have tended to continue with working practices which were adequate pre-1986. This more remote contact with the work of the school is no longer appropriate. The issue of redundancies facing many governing bodies in the summer term 1990 (the first term of delegated budgets for many schools) provides just one example of the need for the governing body to be fully informed about the work of the school. Despite the Secretary of State's announcement that there would be no redundancy as a result of LMS, once schools were notified of their budgets at Easter, governing bodies around the country were involved in making decisions about who to 'let go' and how to do it. (To be fair, the lack of funds may also have been the result of attempts to keep the community charge low at its inception rather than the change to formula funding.) In the author's experience, most of these decisions involved encouraging early retirements or terminating part-time and temporary contracts and thus did not officially count as redundancies, but the distinction is a fine one. Governing bodies must have a clear vision for the future curriculum in their school now that they have the responsibility for taking decisions of this nature.

It is argued that working to an SDP would provide governing bodies with guidelines for the rational deployment of resources within a framework which has general support. Where all involved in the school are given the opportunity to work together in identifying the key areas for development, the problem of decisions being made on the basis of the minimal information known to governors is avoided.

One of the benefits of local financial management is the opportunity to carry forward unspent monies from one year to the next rather than having to 'spend up' by 31st March or lose the funding. This allows schools to manage their funds with a long-term view of the school's development and makes sound planning even more crucial.

Effective ways of working together

Teachers have knowledge about the curriculum and views about how it should develop, governors provide the community's viewpoint to balance that of the professionals. How, then, do these two groups with their different areas of knowledge and responsibility manage the school in the best interests of the children? The answer must lie in developing good lines of communication and effective ways of working.

The amount of time the job takes is a problem for many governors (Deem & Brehony, 1990). There is some feeling that only the retired or those not in full time jobs can carry out the responsibilities adequately. Two self-employed chairs of governors reported spending a day a week in school. How many employers will or can afford to allow employees this latitude? Given the problems of lack of time, expertise and experience, it is not surprising that many governing bodies still maintain their pre-1986 role.

The once-a-term meetings which governors were told to expect are simply not adequate for the job. Governing bodies need to adopt practices and procedures which allow them to be involved in school management at the times when decisions are being made. For instance, if an audit of the school is being carried out to identify areas for development, then the head and governors will need to meet firstly to discuss their concerns and interests, then again, fairly soon afterwards, to draw together the points raised by other interested parties, decide on whole school priorities and the allocation of funds, possible staffing implications and so on. This level of flexibility is essential if the involvement of the governing body is not just to be superficial.

Communicating with parents

The issue of communication with parents is one which many schools were concerned with well before open enrolment, parental access to schemes of work and the requirement for governors to have an annual meeting with parents were placed on the agenda. Yet for many schools it remains a problematic area.

The annual parents' meeting with the governors in its present form appears to be a waste of energy, time and money for most schools. Gibbs (1990) identifies it as the least popular form of parental/school communication. Enough effort has been made for this attempt at accountability to parents to be accepted as inappropriate. Meetings are not often quorate and the curriculum or management of the school are in any case rarely the focus of discussion: popular topics being the quality of school dinners, the uniform and extra-curricular activities. Certainly such meetings should be called where parents or governors see the need but the need for routine meetings in their present form should be questioned.

Gibbs reports that the type of communication parents most welcome is where their child is the focus of the interaction. A meeting with governors, most of whom are not in everyday contact with the children, will never fall into that category. However, many schools report successfully involving parents in development planning. At the very least, the SDP needs to be available to parents and their active support for certain parts of it sought (e.g. home–school liaison issues).

LEAs and HMI

The SDP is likely to be a important document in any inspection whether carried out by the LEA or HMI. Some schools, for instance, establish performance indicators for the work being carried out through the plan and these would clearly form the basis of a dialogue with inspectors over the school's direction. This public nature of the plan does raise issues about content. Can a school afford to acknowledge its weaknesses to such a wide audience?

School development planning is as much about building on strengths as about remedying weaknesses. Nevertheless, the issue of public accountability through the plan does have to be taken seriously and a variety of solutions will be used where sensitive issues are concerned. One thing was clear from the research, SDPs written particularly for an outside audience tend to have little impact in practice.

Conclusion

Heads and governors face a time of changing relationships. The challenges faced by schools in the coming decade 'will test the management skills of governors and headteachers to the full' (Audit Commission, 1988: 3). These skills — in jointly managing the school — will not be acquired without considerable effort on the part of governors and heads. Although working on and to an SDP is not a universal panacea for all the management problems schools will face in the 1990s, the experience of many schools is that the process of producing an SDP encourages the establishment of structures within the school which aid communication and understanding among all the school's partners. Where such structures exist, schools may well become truly locally managed in the best interests of the children of the community.

11 INSET, Professional Development and the Local Management of Schools

ROB McBRIDE

Introduction

Inherent in recent education policy initiatives is the notion that teaching is a rule-following activity. This represents the deprofessionalisation of teaching. Local management of schools (LMS), despite the rhetoric that accompanies it, is in the same tradition though it is argued here that there may be opportunities for teachers to generate professional practice.

INSET

The term INSET has been used to describe a whole range of in-service training activities for teachers, including courses, workshops, conferences, degrees, action research and so on. I recall being part of a Department of Education and Science (DES) funded research project based in one LEA and being told that the LEA saw my visits into schools as free INSET.

Until recently INSET was largely optional. Sometimes a colleague would draw a teacher's attention to a meeting, say at a teachers' centre and she would ask to have time off or she might choose to go down on a Saturday morning. Of course, sometimes a school manager might mention that a meeting was taking place and encourage staff to go and have a look. Indeed I remember being asked from time to time. But over the last 20 years major changes have taken place in what we call INSET.

The James Report (DES, 1972) offered a model of INSET that sought to 'reflect and enhance the status and independence of the teaching profession and of the institutions in which many teachers are educated and trained.' At around the same time the work of Lawrence Stenhouse was influencing the providers of INSET. Stenhouse argued that teachers were crucial not merely to the implementation of the curriculum but also to its development — there could be no curriculum development without teacher development. The development of the curriculum and of teachers were intertwined. For Stenhouse the professional teacher was reflexive of her own practice in collaboration with her colleagues as a researcher, and the unpredictability of this process was valued.

By the mid 1970s the DES and the governments in power began to change their approach to the educational system and in INSET this was signalled by Making INSET Work (DES, 1978a). This small booklet was a report from the Advisory Committee on the Supply and Training of Teachers (ACSTT) which sought 'to rationalise and plan for INSET in a manner which recognises the needs of the system alongside those of the individual teacher' (Harland, 1987).

Further changes came in 1984 when the Advisory Committee on the Supply and Education of Teachers (ACSET, ACSTT recast) argued for an emphasis in institutions on the identification of needs, the training of key personnel, and the evaluation of the institutional effects of training. Using these principles and with a tight control of funding, the government launched TRIST (Technical and Vocational Education Initiative-related INSET) in 1985, under the aegis of the Manpower Services Commission (MSC) as a pilot for GRIST (Grant-related INSET).

GRIST, or the LEA Training Grant Scheme (LEATGS, the formal name) became in effect, the DES policy on INSET and, as explained below, it has had a powerful effect on INSET in schools. The GRIST scheme derived its strategy for teacher development from the Further Education Unit (FEU), an organisation concerned with vocational training where the norm was for young people to be told what was needed for entry to a craft or trade. The FEU advocated curriculum-led staff development, which meant that INSET was a matter of making up the deficit in teaching strengths to ensure the delivery of the curriculum.

Unlike the Stenhouse view, the FEU saw the curriculum as given and delivered rather than developed by teachers. The trend is clear. Stenhouse used the term 'professional development' rather than INSET and it is the meaning of professional development that is discussed in the next section.

Professional Development

Hoyle's (1983) description of professional work is similar to Grundy's

(1990) and to Schon's (1983). According to Hoyle (1983), a professional has to:

- handle non-routine situations, new problems and has to have freedom to make judgements
- be socialised into the values of the professional community, the social practice (see Stenhouse (1975) on this)
- give pre-eminence to clients' interests, interests that are often made explicit in a code of ethics.

In addition,

> the organised profession should have a strong voice in the shaping of relevant public policy, a large degree of control over the exercise of professional responsibilities, and a high degree of autonomy in relation to the state. (Hoyle, 1983: 45).

Centrally, a practitioner is a member of a practice-based community; someone who has been educated in the ways of his or her profession and who exercises judgement in individual situations in the interests of a client. For teachers, that judgement is primarily exercised during the negotiation of the curriculum with her pupils — and this is an inherent part of teaching. Of course, we have all come across those teachers who think they control childrens' minds but it is not so simple.

Some groups or classes of children make it clear that they are going to have a major say in what is taught to them. In most classes it happens much more subtly in that children bring a set of expectations, interests and concerns, and teachers ignore these at their peril. And this is all children, including those apparently neat and tidy middle-class kids who rarely do anything wrong and always complete their homework.

By and large teachers have to keep presenting work that children find appropriate and understandable. Much about the teaching situation rests upon a trusting relationship between teacher and children so that negotiation is not a minute by minute activity nor a confrontational one. The teacher has to account for the needs of individual pupils, although often pupils can be grouped in some way or another for some of the time — the task of providing work for individual pupils is not always an exhausting task. But to summarise, at the heart of the teacher's work is the curriculum — the activities the teacher provides for her pupils and the ways in which this presentation takes place. The curriculum arises from teacher–pupil negotiation and cannot be rigorously preset by detailed national curriculum rules.

Only the teacher is in a position to use her judgement in the interests of her pupils; nobody else is there. Yet this does not give the teacher unlimited freedom to act on her whim, for her perception is guided by her membership of a professional community. At least this is what should be happening. For at present we have no organised body of teachers and no institutional structures to support the teaching profession. We have seen the demise of the Schools' Council which, whatever its weaknesses, gave some support. Ideally we need some kind of teaching council to represent teachers at national level but also to be in touch with local organisations where teachers can engage in professional debate.

It is through that debate, and the consideration of their classrooms, that teachers' professional development could take place. Of course it is not an activity that teachers carry out only with teachers. The teaching profession has to be open to the critical comments of pupils, parents, headteachers, employers, advisers, Local Education Authorities (LEAs) and others. But not to their dictats. And it is not unusual for workers in Britain to be treated in this professional way. There is a long history of groups being trusted to exercise their professional judgement and hence show their initiative. The stock exchange regulates itself, nurses are about to have their work professionalised through Project 2000, the so-called free market has given management professionals much more freedom to manage and there are many other examples. Indeed we live in a professional society and anyone who needs a full account of its history and growth should read Perkin (1989).

Of major concern to those who want a place for professional development is the GRIST policy which encourages a deficit model of INSET. Professional development gives teachers a measure of control over their own practice; it accepts the primacy of the practical wisdom of people who are engaged in their work. Deficit INSET is more about 'experts' identifying the shortfalls and then attempting to put them right by providing a set of rules. Let us consider the current INSET policy.

Current INSET Policy

Since April 1987 INSET policy has been handed down from the DES. Commonly known as GRIST, it has recently been renamed Grants for Education Support and Training, or GEST. It should be seen as one policy among many and so I will briefly comment on the broader context. I add at this point that policy does not necessarily indicate practice though the GRIST policy has been powerful in moulding teacher action.

The lack of a national curriculum organisation for teachers with influence at the DES and deep local roots is one reason why professional development is a scarce activity but it is not the only one. The national curriculum is far too prescriptive and it is meant to be. Many of the details are only there so that the teaching of the curriculum can be tested, so that teachers can be held to account. We have yet to see how demanding the proposed national system of testing is to be but it will lock the national curriculum into place. Whatever is to be tested will be taught and I anticipate that testable knowledge will become more important in schools than whatever might be of most interest to pupils.

We have already seen some retrenchment in the demands of the national curriculum but there is some way to go yet before there is enough leeway for teachers to have sufficient curriculum to develop. But if there were curriculum to be developed teachers would need time to do the work. Currently this is simply not available. To some extent time will mean money, especially for supply cover, although much could be done in other ways that I will outline later.

I have mentioned, but not elaborated upon, the question of funding, probably the instrument of greatest DES control over INSET. As part of GRIST, LEAs have to bid for funds to support the INSET of teachers but the areas of LEA expenditure which are supported by the DES are strictly defined by category. When GRIST began there was a system of local and national priorities, the former giving LEAs some kind of control over their own expenditure. National priorities have increasingly been governed by the needs of the national curriculum and, as we enter the next financial year with GEST, local priorities have been removed altogether.

Categorical funding sets clear limits within which expenditure may take place and for Harland (1987) this type of funding is a substitute for legislation; used by an institution, when it has neither the right nor the means, to implement its own policies.

Needs identification is part of the nomenclature of GRIST. Once a teacher's needs are discerned, the INSET required is defined and, accordingly, it is the tail that wags the INSET dog. The critical question is, who declares the needs of teachers and how is it done? Within the scheme of things teacher appraisal, pupil examination results and adviser/inspector review have been the most frequently mentioned. The problem is that all of these are line management dominated and needs may well not be those of teachers but of the managers and institutions in the system. The practical wisdom of teachers need play no significant part.

Of course, there is no reason why a sensitive form of appraisal might not play an important part in needs identification, a form where peer review was at the centre of the procedure. But it is quite clear that the new Secretary of State for Education intends appraisal to be by managers of their subordinates with all its trappings of power. This is no scenario for honest discussion of a teacher's interests and concerns, more for haughty measurement by the manager and the discrete covering of tracks by the teacher.

A final aspect of GRIST that should be noted is the demand that LEAs should ensure that INSET is cost-effective. This part of the policy has led to sharply reduced opportunities for secondment, less availability of long courses and the growth of short courses or open learning packages. I would not wish to place a blanket criticism upon all short courses but we do not know much about their efficacy and we must surely be concerned at the degree to which financial expediency and management muscle might overtake educational quality.

GRIST has practically nothing to do with professional development but encourages the DES and the government to fund and support the INSET it wants to see. Much of GRIST money pays for national curriculum based INSET but there are also funds available for the education of school managers. This is no surprise for it is to managers in the education service that the central administration looks for the delivery of its policies. The practical wisdom of teachers is of little importance. Any system which ignores teacher judgement based on practical wisdom also ignores professional development. Might LMS offer opportunities for change?

LMS: The Situation Now

The data offered in this section arises from personal research in four LEAs where I have spoken to INSET advisers; from the research that fed into my publication, The In-service Training of Teachers (McBride, 1989); and interviews with my students (practitioners at all levels) and other serving practitioners that my work as a lecturer/researcher brings me into contact with. I do not suggest that the picture I paint is a national one nor a general one, merely the picture I have painted with the data I have received.

Until now, in spite of LMS, all the LEAs I have been into have retained the funding for most INSET. Money for staff development days has been devolved, but funding for INSET remains the mandatory exception to LMS it was originally.

Currently LEAs are under great pressure as they see their educational role being constricted by the devolution of services and funding. Large schools, principally secondary schools, are eager to take on their own INSET budgets. Many schools have annual budgets of over two million pounds, some of which can be vired into INSET. These schools are also able to raise additional funding from parents, local businesses and so on. Yet this is by no means universal and some larger schools, especially in deprived areas or where the catchment area is a widespread rural one without a single sense of community, are still concerned that their share of the LEA INSET budget will not be sufficient to fund reasonable INSET. Small schools, chiefly primary schools, are far less keen to have their own INSET budgets. A primary headteacher recently explained that her INSET budget in a school of 82 children is £95 to cover 'out of county' INSET. Last term two teachers wanted to attend a two and a half day course, the supply cover for which was £375 ($5 \times £75$); £95 only just covered course fees and travelling expenses were still to be found.

I have come across two basic ways that LEAs have devolved INSET funding. The first is simply to give schools a share of the money to spend as they wish. If this were to happen schools would have to decide what their INSET should look like. Would visiting speakers be needed or 'critical friend' advisers from higher education institutions. I recently came across a large school that had spent considerable staff time and effort drawing up its own school development plan but had asked departments to submit their own. It was not until a late stage that it became clear that plans were coming from two directions and were seeking quite different ends. In addition the school had proceeded to plan without having carried out an audit of its strengths and weaknesses. When it finally decided where it wanted to go it became clear that its human resources were not suitable for those sorts of ends and the mess continued to the great consternation of the staff. If INSET is merely a matter of righting deficits to deliver the national curriculum I guess most schools could cope but, as I have indicated, professional development is much more than this, and there is little evidence to suggest that schools have the experience to provide it.

Nevertheless, some professional development could take place if LEAs merely devolved money. Another school has engaged a lecturer to act as critical friend as 12 of its staff research the school and endeavour to improve it. The 12 are all enrolled on an advanced certificate at the University of East Anglia and ultimately they will have brought about considered change and will receive certification for their efforts. It is probable, though, that such a scheme will be beyond the pocket of a small school for the costs per student may well rise where the numbers are smaller.

The second way of devolving funds is aimed partly at making the best of these economies of scale although there are other advantages. Ultimately the pot of money is kept centrally by the LEA and when schools or teachers want funding for INSET they draw up some kind of proposal. Seconded teachers visit proposers for discussion and proposals are gathered together to be considered by a committee made up of teachers, heads, advisers, etc. It is then possible to construct an LEA plan for INSET that provides activities — for minority groups who want unusual inputs; to help schools who may require more INSET than others during, say, a restructuring exercise; to negotiate an improved offer from a provider if numbers wanting INSET are large.

Indeed, the fragmentation that results from devolving all funds, as in the first model above, makes it difficult for providers who have to be in contact with a large number of individuals. Providers also have problems planning for the needs of widely disparate groups and the schools themselves tend to be a little isolated from each other. How would joint ventures such as teachers' centres be funded? The second, devolution of power model, is not without problems in that there are extra bureaucratic costs and the system can be seen as distant and unwieldy if it is not crisply run. Some economies of scale could be taken if schools get together in clusters, as many have done, but this merely gives what has been the LEA role to the schools and a teacher has do the job of co-ordination.

Plainly some kind of mixture of these two schemes, plus others, could provide professional development in an LEA. Interestingly, Smalley (1989) showed how a group of LEAs working together were able to take yet greater economies of scale. He argued strongly that a group of LEAs were able to provide INSET that individual LEAs could not and, moreover, that the bureaucratic cost spread over some ten LEAs added little to the total bill. This is another powerful argument in favour of greater rather than less co-operation between schools and LEAs.

Yet even then the matter is more complex still for, if categorical funding remains, options are limited by the ways in which funding is directed. In this respect is does not matter who spends the money, schools or LEAs.

An INSET adviser has explained to me how little latitude the latest GEST scheme allows. In general LEAs are expected to devolve money under DES guidelines but be accountable for the expenditure. So one part of GEST supports LEAs as they spend on designated courses for science and maths teaching but as the LEA does not have the staff to evaluate the courses they choose not to spend the money on INSET. The adviser claimed that the DES was well aware that many LEAs could not police these courses and that the money would not be devolved.

If more money was devolved to schools, they would be in exactly the same position. As the adviser pointed out he saw a paradox — LEAs and schools were given 'freedom' but were still accountable to the DES.

An additional point is that on visiting LEAs and schools I am frequently assailed by people who tell me that there is so little money that little can be afforded. LEA advisers tell me that when the fixed costs of teachers' centres, INSET for the youth service, further education and others, all of which come from the same budget, are deducted, very little is left. The situation is similar in schools. A headteacher explained that even though his school had a devolved budget under LMS, it was very difficult to make savings in any area except staffing. Staffing typically costs schools over 70% of their budgets and other budgetary items such as energy, rates and so on are now not easily cut. Where economies are made upon the smaller items, the savings are negligible.

If a substantial, useable, sum is to be found the only way of doing it is by cutting staff and that, he felt, was unacceptable educationally. What little he had in his INSET budget was fully taken up taking the pressure off of overworked staff for whom a rest from school was as valuable as any course. The major cost, as ever, was of providing supply cover (if it could be found).

Having a co-ordinating body such as an LEA could enable the taking of economies of scale, planning for minorities, extra support for greater need and provision for minorities. Simple devolution of funds may lead to a 'spread thin' problem, fragmentation and an education system split between large, and wealthy, and small, and poor, schools. It is possible to delegate some power (scheme two) without fragmentation, though it appears that we are not moving in this direction.

LMS and the Future in the Light of the Present

As I have made plain here, we have yet to see the full devolution of INSET funds so this section is in some ways speculative. Nevertheless, I look here at what may come about as more INSET monies are devolved.

I have already referred to the spread-thin problem and the difficulties of providing INSET opportunities for minority groups that would probably be ignored at school level, where they are too thin on the ground. Merely covering the cost of supply teachers is prohibitive as we have seen above. With the simple devolution of money I anticipate that many more long courses for teachers will fold with disastrous effects on universities and other institutions providing higher education. Indeed, how might any providing institution begin to establish what schools and teachers need without some kind of umbrella organisation such as the LEA? One outcome could be that providers go back to running fixed courses that they know will sell well. There may be little incentive for development.

A primary cause for concern is the general demise of the LEA, both as a partner in INSET and more generally. While they have often been the butt of teacher criticism a supportive advisory service, for example, passes on valuable information about INSET to schools and contributes to the LEA INSET picture. A good adviser has knowledge of schools, can help teachers secure the right support and could influence the distribution of funds with school need in mind. If INSET money is devolved on a straight per capita basis, the prospects of imaginative positive discrimination are lost. Should schools spend in an open INSET market we could move into 'consultant' delivered INSET — I have already come across schools that have dipped into this market and soon concluded that, in general, death by a thousand consultants is slickly presented but boring and expensive. In addition, LEA officers can handle the time-consuming administration and negotiation that attends the organisation of professional development.

Yet as I have already indicated, INSET takes place within a rigid framework and what appears to be an opportunity for free choice is not so in practice. The next section looks at this framework and considers whether some form of professional development might be possible.

The GRIST Framework and the Potential for Professional Development

If anything gives me a modicum of hope it is the Kettering Alternative Approach (KAA) as described by Tim Bartlett (1989). This is a story of six secondary schools in an ordinary Midland town that rejected competition and instead put ceilings on their intakes to avoid competition. They formed a central unit for curriculum development and, according to both Bartlett and an external team of evaluators (Simons, Elliott & MacDonald, 1988), the quality of curriculum development was of a good standard. Teachers were seconded for variable periods to carry out the wishes of groups of teachers within the schools. In short, teachers had a measure of control over the curriculum with community involvement and resourcing for professional development. To some extent the individual needs of teachers emanating from their classroom-based judgements could be satisfied. Partly due to the onset of GRIST, the scheme folded, the GRIST framework helped kill the scheme.

There are three central pillars to GRIST, the national curriculum, associated tests and categorical funding. It does not end there for, within the policy, cost-effectiveness is demanded. Yet at all levels collaboration is expected. Now, collaboration is a slippery concept; it is possible to collaborate on all sorts of bases but, as rhetoric, it has proved powerful. The rhetoric of the the associated issue of 'freedom' offered to schools is of the same kind. It is a fake freedom and is the sort of freedom rooted in the ideas of Hayek which runs through much of the approach of our current government.

Hayek (1960) made three critical distinctions, between: liberty and democracy; law and bureaucracy; the market and planning. Liberty was more important than democracy in that individuals should be able to operate without the influence of others. Strong laws were required to ensure that this individual libertarianism was protected and bureaucratic organisations were subject to the same laws to keep them at arms length too. The market was the sphere of voluntary individual behaviour, regulated by law and free from the intrusion of the planning tendency of bureaucracies.

The GRIST framework is very similar to the application of such a philosophy. The great weakness is that neither teachers nor their organisations, such as they are, have had the opportunity to influence the strong laws. At the DES, bureaucracy has been cut away and LEAs are being pared back. But in schools there are reams of paperwork to be filled in before INSET can take place and, as headteachers in schools well know, LMS and GRIST are paper nightmares. In other words, the DES cannot see it but there is plenty of evidence of bureaucracy at the school level.

While the strong laws of GRIST and LMS exist, expressed through the curriculum, testing and categorical funding, professional development is rarely seen. The KAA is a distant dream.

Harold Perkin (1989) has argued that we live in a professional society, the central feature of which has been the conflict between professionals in the private sector and those, such as teachers, in the public sector. Currently the private sector professionals, and above all management professionals, have hegemony in this battle. The outcome is that management is calling the tune and the goals being set for teaching professionals reflect the values of managers, not the sort of values reflected in the practical wisdom of teachers. Accordingly, quantifiable data such as examination results and financial information dominates what teachers value. Broadly, the practical wisdom of teachers sees a place for creativity, understanding, open-ended argument, reflection, self evaluation and similar 'soft' non-quantifiable notions.

These aspects of the curriculum may well not be valued if we push ahead with a fixed and detailed curriculum that is hammered into place by summative testing and published examination results. Professional development will not be more desirable if headteachers are seen as being responsible for the imposed outcomes seen as desirable by the DES. Managers in schools will be visibly responsible for delivering the national curriculum and INSET will be the medicine for teachers who cannot deliver the examination results. Any teacher who had the misfortune to go through the cascade that accompanied the introduction of GCSE will know that INSET of this kind is a waste of time and money, made doubly worse because it sees the interests and concerns of teachers as irrelevant.

It would be easy to dismiss this analysis as negative and gloomy. I reject such responses. I believe that those who refuse to confront this negative situation are those who are irrelevant to the future. Suppressing an unpleasant scenario makes teachers much less able to represent themselves and their values. As the managers say, we need to be proactive rather than reactive. We need to understand what is wrong and stand up for the values of teachers if professional development rather than cheap INSET is to be a reality.

Attempting to take a lead is difficult while we remain fragmented in the absence of an influential national organisation of teachers. But look at the hopeful signs.

I am already finding considerable subversion in schools of the rules and regulations that hinder teacher professionalism. For example, I was recently in a school that wanted to develop drama as a cross-curriculum subject, but the only money it could find was directed to a national curriculum subject. After considerable staff discussion it was decided to have a drama day but call it something appropriate. Ultimately the practical wisdom of teachers will keep finding ways of expressing itself and, as long as it is in the interests of children and carefully debated, surely it is defensible.

LMS, despite my criticisms of it, offers opportunities for subversion. As the education system has been re-formed, the DES and the government have built in checking mechanisms to attempt to ensure that policies are put into practice. These include HMI, local LEA advisers (see McBride, 1989: ch. 5), national assessment and categorical funding. But as MacIntyre (1981: 101) has written:

> What the totalitarian project will always produce will be a kind of rigidity and inefficiency which may contribute in the long run to its defeat. . . . But that rebuttal entails also a large rejection of the claims of what I called bureaucratic managerial expertise. . . . The expert's claim to status and reward is fatally undermined when we recognise that he [*sic*] possesses no sound stock of law-like generalisations and when we realise

how weak the predictive power available to him is. (MacIntyre, 1981: 101)

I expect that teachers will gradually find ways of putting into place supportive and sensitive forms of appraisal, and action research, and begin to interpret the national curriculum in ways that help their pupils to develop. The more proactive teachers are, the less opportunity for the curriculum government and curriculum police to re-create education according to their alien values. Of course, we cannot be demanding for teachers are feeling overwhelmed and undervalued, but eventually I believe that they will win back their professionalism.

12 Towards a Systematic Management of Professional Staff Development in Schools[1]

HUGH BUSHER

The Background to the New Style INSET

The process of staff development has changed drastically in the last seven years. Until 1983 the organisation of staff development was in the hands of the providers — LEAs and institutions of higher education. Teachers' needs were identified only on the basis of providers' historic experiences, and the organisational needs of schools were not considered at all.

The James Report (DES, 1972) recommended that teacher education should go through three cycles, the last of which would ensure the continued growth of professional understanding throughout a teacher's working life. This notion was taken up by the Advisory Committee on the Supply and Training of Teachers (ACSTT) but modified by it in its report 'Making INSET work' (DES, 1978). This report suggested that INSET programmes should recognise the needs of schools as well as those of teachers.

However, little was done. In the intervening years between 1978 and 1986, LEAs seem to have made little effort to introduce systematic schemes of INSET. Jones, O'Sullivan & Reid (1987) comment on the lack of research data on patterns of INSET before the mid 1980s, although a study was carried out by Cane (1969) into teachers' views and preferences for in-service training, and Donoughue et al. (1981) edited a collection of papers for the Open University about various aspects of LEA supported INSET.

The earliest attempt at a systematic provision of INSET which gave weight to both the needs of teachers and those of the organisation was the Technical Vocational Educational Initiative, (TVEI)-related in-service programme (TRIST), which ran from 1985–7. Saunders (1986), in his evaluation of eight TRIST projects, notes that one of the key features differentiating TRIST from LEA organised INSET was that the former constructed courses to satisfy the identified needs of schools taking part in TVEI, while the latter pursued a more *ad hoc* approach, offering courses which it hoped some teachers would find interesting and, so, would attend. McBride (1989) argues that TRIST was deliberately set up as a pilot scheme to introduce LEAs to needs-driven INSET, though Saunders disagrees.

There was no entitlement of access to INSET courses for teachers. In Cane's (1969) study of in-service short course provision in Durham, Norfolk and Glamorgan, between 50% and 72% of teachers attended courses. Yet 80% of teachers said that they positively wanted in-service training. It would seem that one major reason for teachers not attending courses was the views of headteachers.

> In my experience in some schools you got on an [in-service] course if your face fitted, or if the head wanted you to go. . . . At another school I worked in, the headteacher [thought he] knew exactly what people wanted and how he saw people's futures, so he knew exactly which courses to put in pigeon holes for certain people. (Staff tutor, Interview, 1987)

Headteachers played an important gatekeeping role in controlling teachers' access to such courses, both in making known to teachers what courses were available and in supporting teachers' applications to their LEA for funding to pay fees and travelling expenses.

Nor was there any mechanism for giving priority funding to one area or type of INSET in preference to any other. The DES encouraged the professional development of teachers by paying the fees for long term award bearing courses out of the uncapped pool, so long as the courses were run by an accredited institution of higher education. However, there appears to have been no attempt to decide systematically which courses should be supported in preference to other courses. Nor was there any attempt to evaluate the impact of these courses on school processes. As the number of secondments or attendances on long courses rose, so did DES contributions. Since teachers studied for these courses either during their private time after school or during one term (or longer) secondments, costs of money and time severely curtailed access to them, as well as headteachers' views.

The staff training element of INSET (i.e. school-focused short courses on how to carry out practice) before the mid 1980s was provided through LEA-run, in-house courses for teachers. Some of these were award bearing, at least in the sense that the LEA gave a certificate, but many of them were not. Staffordshire, for example, ran a large number of short courses at its teachers' centres for updating teachers' professional knowledge.

The New Style INSET

The first steps to create a needs-driven approach to LEA provided teacher professional development were taken in 1983. In that year, under Circular 3/83 (DES, 1983), central government initiated a limited scheme of categorically funded INSET by sponsoring 20 one-day management courses, for senior teachers in schools at named provider institutions of higher education. The intention of this scheme was to begin to meet the identified needs of schools to have senior teachers who were adequately trained to manage schools.

With the publication of Circular 6/86 (DES, 1986) and the Education (Training Grants) Regulations (1987a), the DES expanded this scheme and established its financial control over INSET programmes. This scheme, the Local Education Authority Training Grants (LEATGs), scheme, was fiercely needs led and financially guided. On the one hand it limited the extent of LEA autonomy in planning INSET programmes, both by tying the level of funding for INSET courses to DES criteria, and by insisting that LEAs carry out an audit of the in-service needs of their schools and teachers before bidding for DES funding. To further constrain LEAs, the pooling arrangements were abandoned and TRIST was scrapped. On the other hand, LEAs were now free to run courses at any institution they chose, since, under the LEATGS the DES no longer specified which courses at which institutions were acceptable for financial support from government grants.

Its purpose was to:

- promote the professional development of teachers
- promote the systematic and purposeful planning of in-service training
- encourage the more efficient management of the teaching force
- encourage training in selected areas which are given a national priority.
  (DES, 1986)

In this scheme the need for balance referred to by ACSTT (DES, 1978), between teachers' individual needs and school institutional needs, seems to have swung heavily in favour of the institution. Indeed, Wright (1987) argued that the style of the new INSET no longer treats teachers as professionals because it emphasises the training of teachers through short courses to meet the identified needs of their schools. However, this is to overlook the numbers of teachers undertaking B.Phil, higher degrees, and other institutionally accredited professional qualifications. It is also to overlook the range of different types of knowledge which, say, Eraut (1988) considers it necessary for professional teachers to have to carry out their work effectively.

This paper attempts to address the question of how INSET is coming to be managed within this changed administrative framework in order to deliver needs driven programmes of staff development.

Sources of Data used to Explore these Issues

The data is drawn from three pieces of ethnographic research, which all date from the academic year 1987/88. The first is a conference for secondary school staff tutors and inexperienced teachers on inducting new teachers into school. This took place in Leeds in the autumn of 1987. The views of ten staff tutors and eight inexperienced teachers were recorded.

The second source of data is a discussion with 50 staff tutors in secondary schools in a northern LEA attending a course in the spring and summer of 1988 on how to manage staff development in schools. Handwritten notes were kept of the main points emerging in each discussion.

The third source of data is the returns of staff tutors from 21 secondary schools in Midshire to the LEA on what INSET courses were being run in their schools in the academic year 1987/88.

The Need for a More Systematic Approach to INSET

The pressure towards a more systematic approach to managing INSET came both from the changing administrative framework of education instigated by central government in the mid 1980s and from teachers' school based concerns to exercise more sophisticated control over school processes.

The curriculum reforms instigated by the establishment of GCSE (in 1986) and enacted through the Education Reform Act (1988) generated a need for all teachers to be involved in programmes of staff development. The new management framework for schools created by the Education (No. 2) Act (1986) and by the Education Reform Act (1988) increased the need for programmes of staff development. These initiatives made it necessary for schools to find ways of identifying and prioritising teachers' and schools' needs, since it was unlikely that everybody could attend every course which they needed to at the same time. The pressure towards a more systematic approach to managing INSET was enhanced by the Teachers' Pay and Conditions Act (1987) which extended the school teachers' working year from 190 days to 195 days, allocating the extra five days to staff development.

Within schools, some teachers wanted to facilitate school development. They shared the view expressed by Lyons (1976) that staff development was a central aspect of a headteacher's task if he or she wanted to promote school development. Wideen & Andrews (1987) came to the same conclusion, that school improvement was impossible without staff development.

Some teachers wanted to have greater control over their own decisions and felt they could achieve this by continually enhancing their professional knowledge. Staff tutors in Leeds in 1987 offered two reasons for involving all teachers in staff development programmes. One was a professional argument that teachers were made not born and had always to be thinking how they could improve the quality of education which pupils were experiencing.

The other was a recognition that teachers were institutionalised professionals and, as employees, needed to understand the system within which they were working:

> Entering a new job, anything which takes over your life is quite a major transition . . . you've got kids at one end and your colleagues. You're a professional in your classroom — an authority, and you have to be — but you're an employee outside, subordinate and junior to the deputy head, the hierarchy. (Staff tutor, Interview, 1987)

The entitlement to staff development, which the Teachers' Pay and Conditions Act (1987) guaranteed and which the other innovations demanded, appears to have raised the status of INSET in the perceptions of some teachers from an unseemly scramble for career advancement to an essential element of professional practice:

> Staff development was in danger at one time of meaning teacher promotion. One talked about staff development in terms of having interviews to decide how your career was going to progress. What we've talked about today is largely professional people developing better in doing their classroom job better. That is encouraging. (Staff tutor, Interview, 1987)

Managing the New Style INSET — The Internal School Processes

Several staff tutors emphasised the need for schools to have a staff development policy, so that people in the school as well as clients of the school — such as parents and employers — knew that it was taking place in a systematic manner:

> I have a very firm belief that within a large school . . . there has to be a school policy, an agreed and understood consensus . . . It's a case of presenting a coherent picture to everybody else, including parents and children. (Staff tutor, Interview, 1987)

It was also important to have a staff development policy in place so that teachers could see that the school was prepared to commit resources to it. Busher (1990) points out the importance of organisations committing resources to the processes of change as well as to the outcomes of change if change is to be successfully implemented:

> Because it is important to have policies, I always get my headteacher to state that she/he will support any in-service training. That's a nice easy policy, with a caveat, providing we can get cover. (Staff tutor, Interview, 1987)

The financial resources to support supply cover come from two sources. One is a school's general budget. The other is from the LEATGS, when the cause of teachers' absence can be attributed to their attendance on central government/LEA approved training courses. The actual amount which schools can provide for supply cover seems to vary enormously, with £70 per teacher per year being, apparently, the least that is available.

In discussing how school-focused staff development policy is being managed, staff tutors developed descriptions which can be grouped under several subheadings:

- the leadership of the staff development policy
- the membership of a staff development committee
- the delegated powers of a staff development committee
- the administrative functions of a staff development committee

Leadership of a staff development policy

Most of the people interviewed thought that a staff development programme should be co-ordinated by a person of deputy head status. This was for two reasons. Firstly, so that he or she wielded sufficient power in order to be able to enact policy. Secondly, so that he or she was able to be part of the central policy-making process through his or her membership of the leading coalition (senior management team, in managerial terms):

> The higher the status a staff tutor has, the easier it is to do the job. Although the best person to be staff tutor is the most sympathetic person in the school, in reality you need power — like the deputy head who has been designated as staff tutor (Staff tutor, Interview, 1988)

One staff tutor pointed out what value it was to her work to be also the school timetabler. She could ensure that the probationary teachers' induction programme was not eaten into by demands for internal supply cover.

Staff tutors saw themselves as having a very wide role — indeed, one thought it impossible to combine successfully this role with that of classroom teacher: 'All matters to do with staff welfare, development, INSET, students, probationers, eventually appraisal' (Staff tutor, Interview, 1987)

The emergence of compulsory INSET days has further widened their brief.

Staff tutors appeared to operate in four different but overlapping domains. These are: the domain of school-wide policy making through the discussions of the leading coalition; the domain of staff development committee deliberations — where such a body exists; the domain of interdepartmental and interpersonal interaction; and the domain of interschool liaison and the maintenance of other external links.

In the first domain of school policy making, as a member of the school's leading coalition, staff tutors expected both to be able to guide the staff development programme and to be able to influence that coalition in supporting a programme of staff development.

In the second domain, staff tutors saw their role as that of chairperson and co-ordinator and, as member and representative of the leading coalition, expected to be able to interpret school policy to a staff development committee, where such a body existed.

In the third domain, staff tutors' performance seemed to have several aspects. One of these was liaising with heads of department and helping them to create departmental policies for staff development which integrated with whole school policies: 'Part of my role as staff tutor ought to be working with heads of department rather than just dealing with individuals. It is setting structures departmentally' (Staff tutor, Interview, 1988).

While this aspect had many creative functions, it also had a trouble-shooting function. Some non-promoted teachers seemed to regard staff tutors as being a 'court of appeal' against unsuccessful supervision by heads of department:

> It is an extremely difficult situation having to try to talk to the head of department. In the end I just had to pluck up the courage and say [of a probationary teacher] 'Look, she is really unhappy. She doesn't feel she has got a relationship with you, and we need to talk.' We had a very difficult session and it [the situation] didn't improve immediately. (Staff tutor, Interview, 1987).

A second aspect of their performance in this third domain was that of involving other teachers in contributing to staff development programmes, especially when such involvement might encourage entrenched teachers to begin a journey of professional development:

> Certain members of staff felt terribly undervalued . . . and they saw all these changes and saw it as implicit criticism . . .

> If you are running in-service courses, you pull in resources from the rest of the staff . . .

> [It] does amazing things for morale because it demonstrates that you value their experience and their expertise.
> (Staff tutor, Interview, 1988)

In the fourth domain of external liaison, staff tutors described their work as having several aspects. One of these, conventionally perhaps, was to oversee the induction programmes of probationary and student teachers. Another was to instigate and facilitate staff development programmes based on clusters of schools — a group of schools in relatively close geographical proximity to each other. The Midshire staff tutors perceived this as an important aspect of their role, because it enhanced the range of provision of courses and support for teachers, largely through working parties for curriculum development, beyond that which any one school could provide on its own.

Membership of a staff development committee

Implicitly and explicitly in their discussions staff tutors considered that a staff development programme should be constructed by a staff committee with a delegated authority from the headteacher. The extent and nature of that delegation are considered in the next section.

> It's a horrible term 'the hierarchy' . . . we are all teachers in that school.
> There ought to be an open management structure whereby we can talk to
> one another and give praise and recognition to whoever is doing well.
> (Staff tutor, Interview, 1988)

Staff tutors perceived this involvement of teachers as positively beneficial to a
school, while acknowledging that it posed risks to the authority of senior staff,
particularly those who preferred to work in an autocratic manner. Both
Conway (1978) and Day (1985) considered that the degree to which teachers
participate in schools' decision making correlates positively with their level of
satisfaction with school management:

> Give the staff a chance to be involved. Don't keep it all at top
> management level . . . if you trust your staff then things will evolve . . .

> There are managerial dangers in how much power you devolve, but you
> get a great resonse from staff . . . (Staff tutor, Interview, 1988).

The involvement of other teachers on a staff development committee also
gave senior staff considerable support both in feeling part of a team and in
sharing the workload of organising staff development: 'When I did the work
last year, there were eight of us and it was great because I didn't feel so
exposed. When it was deciding how to plan it we thrashed it out as a group
(Staff tutor, Interview, 1987). One school reported that it had a probationer
and an inexperienced teacher on its committee and felt this to be most
valuable.

The delegated powers of a staff development committee

This section and the next one, on the administrative functions of a staff
development committee, form part of the same debate about what is the
function of a such a committee. This section considers political questions
about the weight of authority which such a committee might wield. The next
considers instrumental questions of how staff development programmes are
organised.

Opinion among senior teachers on this subject was divided, but there
appeared to be a continuum of types of staff development committee which
ranged from, at the least powerful end, the advisory model to, at the most
powerful end, the policy-making subcommittee (analogous to a statutory
committee of an LEA).

In the advisory model, the staff development committee was a
consultative body to the head and senior teachers which suggested what

programmes might be created, and how they might be run (time of day; people involved). Although it had responsibility for sounding out staff opinion and a limited responsibility for organising courses and meetings, in practice, in this model, much of the organising and liaising was actually done by the staff tutor. If it had a budget, this was allocated by the senior management team, with categories of expenditure clearly defined.

In such a model the head and senior management dominated. Several staff tutors made the point that such a model did not challenge the power of the head, and so did not make heads feel uneasy. Others suggested that heads had to feel very secure in their dominance of a school before they would be willing to have their policies questioned by a more proactive staff development committee.

A second model which some staff tutors described was that of a committee which functioned rather like an academic department. It had delegated power to act within a limited sphere of competence, under the oversight of a staff tutor, usually a deputy head. Certain aspects of school policy were within its remit. It might organise, for example, an annual audit of teacher's perceptions of their in-service needs, either through discussion or through questionnaire or, perhaps, through a school review process like GRIDS (McMahon *et al.*, 1984).

> After soliciting requests and information from staff, I go to a card index and make a note and cross refer. There are some surprising people you find . . . who want to go to careers, or want guidance . . . so that when information comes in about a course it won't just be given to the people doing the job anyway. (Staff tutor, Interview, 1987).

Such a committee would draw up a programme to meet the needs so identified by teachers, as well as the needs identified by other means by the head and other senior teachers, and present this to the head sitting in council with the senior management of the school, to gain authority to implement the programme.

The deputy head (staff tutor) would argue the case for the programme in meetings of the senior management team. Several staff tutors pointed out that it was the necessity of liaison between committee and senior management of this sort, which made it very difficult for a staff tutor to operate effectively if he or she did not have membership of the senior management team (leading coalition).

Despite the delegated authority which a committee in this model had, its power was tightly circumscribed. Not only could the senior management team control its programme through debating and determining its budget but, staff tutors suggested, it would probably not be able to question the validity or importance of needs identified by a headteacher. Where such needs clashed with those identified by other teachers, it seems likely that a head's priorities would be given preference.

A few staff tutors gave evidence of a third model of a staff development committee, that of a policy making subcommittee of the school decision-making process. The crucial difference between this model and either of the others, was that the head's authority of office (Watson, 1969) was subject to the same bureaucratic authority (Weber, 1960) created by the procedural rules recommended by the subcommittee (and accepted by the decision-making processes of the school) as were requests for support put forward by any other teacher.

The committee's authority manifested itself in its having a delegated budget, for which it had to argue at management meetings, but which it could then spend according to criteria which it had drawn up and made public. In some cases the committee considered not only which in-service courses to provide in school, but also teachers' requests to attend courses and meetings outside school: 'If six people apply for the same course, then we negotiate. If some people are disappointed, it's recorded and they will get priority later' (Staff tutor, Interview, 1988). In one case, a staff tutor told of a headteacher's request for money to attend a meeting being turned down because the meeting fell outside the priorities for staff development which had been drawn up and agreed by teachers through the staff development committee.

The administrative functions of staff development committees

This section deals with what is involved in organising staff development. Staff tutors described four major elements in this. These were budgeting and managing resources; preparing and implementing a programme to meet identified needs; facilitating social interaction among staff; and working with other schools and other institutions.

Budgeting varied considerably in sophistication from one school to another and had two aspects, a financial aspect and a non-financial aspect. In some schools financial budgeting meant little more than collecting money from staff to pay for coffee or to pay for lunches provided during in-service 'Baker Days'. In other schools, it was left to the staff tutor, alone or in discussion with the staff development committee, to allocate the school INSET budget between guest speakers and other activities, and to consider under what headings the school could apply to the LEA for categorical funds under the LEATGS. Some staff tutors in Midshire had been able to use such categorical funds to buy in supply cover when this was directly related to releasing teachers for INSET courses which fell under DES or LEA priorities.

The availability of supply cover is a problem bedevilling the organisation of daytime in-service programmes: 'Because it is important to have policies . . . . That's a nice easy policy, with a caveat, providing we can get cover' (Staff tutor, Interview, 1987). Some schools were working together to share the costs of running INSET programmes and, at the same time finding other advantages in providing INSET on a cluster basis, as is discussed below.

The non-financial aspect of managing resources had several facets. One of these was finding the most appropriate means of supplying expertise to support whatever needs had been identified. Some of this expertise already lay within the schools:

> If you are running in-service courses, you pull in resources from the rest of the staff. There is nothing entrenched people like more than to find you want them to speak and you value what they have to say. (Staff tutor, Interview, 1988)

As this quotation makes clear, using existing expertise in a school enhanced the professional development of both the giver and the receivers.

Another facet was finding a suitable time for teachers to be involved in INSET. Foremost of staff tutors' concerns here was the impact on pupils' learning which frequent teacher absences might have. Staff tutors sought to minimise this problem by organising INSET, when possible, at times when teachers were not in contact with classes. However, this then meant that marking and preparation time was disrupted. Often, staff tutors found that they had no alternative but to take teachers out of lessons and employ supply teachers to have contact with the pupils.

The second element of administering INSET was that of preparing and implementing a staff development programme to meet identified needs. The identification of needs seems to have been carried out in a variety of ways, from the very formal use of LEA identification of needs forms to the relatively informal, including suppositions by staff tutors about what people might need, made on the basis of their historic experiences:

> This term we have had ten new staff and I have organised an induction programme that is part of directed time. It lasts until Christmas. At the first meeting I outlined the sort of thing I thought would be helpful — such as pastoral care; new initiatives in school; parent consultations; records of achievement . . . Each time we meet we discuss the agenda for the next meeting. (Staff tutor, Interview, 1987)

The term 'programme' has to be understood very broadly here. It not only included long and short courses both school-based and off-school site, but it also included attendance at meetings and workshops, as well as one-to-one counselling sessions, and the briefing of certain temporary categories of teachers in a school such as supply teachers and student teachers:

> I do think it is extremely important to have an up-to-date staff handbook. I think it is helpful to new staff. So that at the front there is a list of staff names as well as information like the room the person usually teaches in, the form they have, the subjects they teach, their role in school. (Staff tutor, Interview, 1988)

The third element, considered by many staff tutors to be as important as managing the formal processes, was the facilitating of social interaction amongst staff. Some of this was formally organised:

> One of the things I have done is, in the first couple of weeks of a new term, to always arrange a social out of school in a pub and invited as many people as possible. If senior staff see colleagues out of the school environment it is useful for all of us, particularly the new staff. (Staff tutor, Interview, 1987)

Sometimes it was informal and low key:

> Just having the opportunity to say how how you feel and talk about what is happening . . . and share your anxieties and, hopefully, get some supportive feedback is incredibly important. It is much better if there is a group of you because other people can say 'I found that too'. (Staff tutor, Interview, 1987)

It is within this context that many staff tutors emphasised the importance of providing a sociable lunch during 'Baker' in-service days.

The fourth element was that of working with other schools and other institutions. One dimension of this was working with higher education. A second dimension was that of close liaison with the LEA:

> Another thing that is quite important is to get the school's adviser in very quickly so that he or she can meet the probationary teachers before they come to observe them. When I was a young teacher, I was scared to death at the thought of an adviser coming in. (Staff tutor, Interview, 1988)

Midshire tutors also involved advisers in organising cluster based courses and workshops. These seemed to be part of a partnership in which advisers and staff tutors worked together to meet the needs which they had variously identified. In some cases, these were needs which were supported by national priority categories under the LEATGS. In addition, staff tutors could use centrally organised Midshire courses either to support school development needs — e.g. preparing for LMS — or to meet identified personal needs of teachers which were too costly for individual schools to provide — e.g. preparing for retirement, a few teachers in widely scattered schools.

Another dimension was that of working with other neighbouring schools. This occurred at two levels in the school hierarchy. At the higher level, staff tutors gained support and succour from working with each other: 'The only way that we are going to get support is to work professionally, with our own professional network of support' (Staff tutor, Interview, 1987).

In some LEAs such practices had originally developed through TVEI clusters. In other cases they seemed to have grown up from LEA initiatives or by chance, through local schools talking with each other.

[The LEA] is very good on initiatives . . . they did a pilot scheme in about half a dozen schools developing professional tutors . . . the notion of the staff tutor became LEA policy. At the end of one staff tutors' conference . . . we decided to formalise the staff tutors' network. (Staff tutor, Interview, 1987)

At a lower level in the school hierarchy, cluster based activities infused many parts of schools' staff development programmes. In Midshire most programmes described many teachers attending area-based subject meetings or curriculum workshops, in part to meet the demands of implementing GCSE, in part to meet national and local priority categories of staff development.

Reflections — What Staff Tutors did Not Say

In this last section, I consider whether the new schemes of INSET enhance or diminish teacher professionality, or bring our conceptions of it into a new focus.

While many teachers are still attending B-Phil. and higher degree courses, often at their own expense, the Midshire school staff development programmes, under the financial impulsion of the LEATGS, were largely made up of short courses, meetings and workshops. Many of these lasted no longer than half a day, though some had several such sessions throughout the academic year. The induction courses run by the Leeds staff tutors, were of a similar nature, as were those school-based courses described by the staff tutors from the Northern LEA.

While these courses were intended to meet teachers' needs and, in

Midshire, these were needs identified by the teachers, none the less these needs were to do with institutional imperatives of helping schools to cope with changes in the environment (see, for example, DES, 1986). Far from achieving a balance between school needs and individual needs, recommended by ACSTT (DES, 1978), the new schemes of INSET weigh organisational needs for changes in teacher knowledge more heavily than individual needs for a deeper understanding of pedagogic processes. It is this which may have led McBride (1989: 9) to describe the LEATGS as 'plac[ing] the teaching profession in a cage'.

Yet it is difficult to conceptualise the creation of an entitlement to staff development (under the 1987 Teachers' Pay and Conditions Act), even though the emphasis of programmes appears to be on organisational needs, as a decline in teacher professionality. Eraut (1988) points out that as teachers progress through their careers they need to acquire a range of management knowledge. Wilkinson & Cave (1988) point out that the process of teaching involves that of managing, whether it be managing pupils or managing teachers and other adults. Since schools are organisations, as Paisey (1981) elaborates, this is scarcely surprising. But it underscores the conception of teachers as institutionalised professionals, rather than as loose associations of autonomous individuals. Consequently, the acquisition of knowledge to resolve institutional problems can be interpreted as the acquisition of professional knowledge, and not merely as staff training in how to carry out practices.

Staff development programmes which focus on organisational needs then enhance teacher professional knowledge, not lessen it, although that enhancement may be in only one area of knowledge — organisational processes — which is relevant to teachers' work. Other areas might be, for example, curriculum development; assessment and testing; self-knowledge and knowledge of other people.

This interpretation of the new schemes of INSET is enhanced by two features in the Midshire schools' programmes of staff development. Many of the 'courses' which Midshire teachers attended were concerned with the construction of the curriculum, and did not focus merely on how to run the administrative system. Many of the area-based 'courses' were workshops in which teachers pooled their existing knowledge and tried to construct new patterns of knowledge, albeit to help their schools and their pupils meet the changing educational environment. But then that is the type of activity, of practitioners' using their knowledge and judgement to resolve new problems in the interests of their clients, which Schon (1983), among many others would conceive as evidence of professional activity.

Note

1. Paper given at the BERA Seminar on the Local Management of Schools, Derbyshire College of Higher Education, Mickleover, Derby, 1st November 1990.

13 The Paradoxes in the Management of Education

GWEN WALLACE

Introduction

This chapter stands as a postscript to the papers presented earlier. My aim is to draw together and locate some of the paradoxes that have emerged.

In order to do this, I shall return to the point I made in Chapter 1 that the 1988 Education Reform Act (ERA) has established a centrally defined and managed structure of financial limits within which schools must self-manage locally. The limits are not, of course, merely financial. If they were, schools would be given their formula funded budget and left to fend for themselves, in the market for pupils, without further government interference. Instead, the government has legislated for a structure of accountability using the national curriculum, standardised assessment, and open access; where open access operates in a context of a new diversity of provision which includes the possibility for schools to opt out of local authority control into grant maintained status, and the setting up of city technology colleges.

This structure is far from fixed and has already been modified in a variety of ways since 1988 by subsequent decrees from the Secretary of State. Nevertheless centrally defined criteria for funding, curricula, assessment and access constitute the legislative framework within which schools are required to function. In combination, all of these measures are portrayed as radical innovations designed to raise educational standards.

Given the importance of the issue of assessment and 'standards' in the debate, and the way in which standards are portrayed as major objectives for the new, locally managed schools, it is worth developing two points: first, that national assessment will not help parents to choose schools, and second, that assessment processes contain paradoxes and dilemmas which stem from the difference in perspective of educationists as against commercial managers.

These in turn are reflected in the paradoxes built into local management. I shall then set out some of the key dimensions of the local management process which illustrate this and argue that the issues are about management, not about parental choice.

Bottom Up or Top Down?

If we leave out the human factor and locate the interests of organisational managers in a process of information gathering and decision making, aimed at ensuring that the purposes of the organisation are effectively and efficiently pursued, then we have to ask for what purposes the information gained from assessment will be used. What kind of decisions might managers make based on the results of the programmes for testing children at 7, 11, 14 and 16? This question has been somewhat obscured by the rhetoric that has portrayed standardised testing as a way of providing information to parents from which they might make a suitable choice of school. The 'parent as consumer' model suggests that schools which can publish good results will attract pupils away from schools with less good results, ultimately making them non-viable businesses, even though pupils' academic attainments represent only one aspect of a school's reason for existence, and parents can learn little about a school from its crude assessment results. So I will take parent power first to clear the ground for the management issues.

Parent power rests on the principle of consumer choice of school. Parents themselves have been reported as mystified by the notion (Nash, 1990). We do know however, that urban parents who can afford to, tend to avoid the more run-down neighbourhoods, purchasing property marked by house agents as being in a 'good area' for schools. We also know that schools tend to be neighbourhood schools, reflecting the socio-economic power of their intake. This is not to ignore the growing evidence that socio-economic circumstances do not *determine* school effectiveness.

We also have reports which suggest that parents cannot assume the luxury of open choice, in spite of open access. There are heads who, faced with too many potential pupils, have become the arbiters of pupil prospects, deciding whom to keep and whom to send elsewhere. It is already apparent that the game is not being played on a level field. Middle-class areas already boast schools which can attract parental cash as well as the cultural capital parents pass on to their children. These are the schools which are most likely to start and stay at the top of any league of overall results on national tests. Open access is unlikely to challenge them at all. If there is any change, it will operate to exclude marginal pupils who do not fit well with the middle-class norms, rather than the reverse. This argument has also been set up as elitism versus egalitarianism, where some elitists accuse an unidentified egalitarian, educationist 'establishment' of envy (Sexton, 1990). Another way of putting it is to say that the debate is about resource distribution and opposed interests. If, as the government is advocating, more schools opt out of local authority control, then the way is open for the age-weighted pupil formula to be replaced by a standard voucher that can be 'topped up' by parental contributions. Is it possible that a school system geared to differential spending in a way that benefits the financially powerful can possibly make for a broader consumer choice, raised standards and professional accountability? As it stands, the evidence suggests that 'choice' will be a luxury to be paid for and that choice in the market for schools will simply reinforce and legitimate differential resourcing of schools in favour of the already well-endowed. Test results from middle-class neighbourhood schools will merely tell parents what they already know.

There is less scope too for parents who wish to work collectively to change the school their pupils already attend, in spite of their majorities on governing boards, although there are examples of schools collaborating for their mutual benefit and drawing parents in from the community. However, the lobbying by the National Association of Parent Teachers Associations (PTAs) for the mandatory provision of a PTA in every school, which just might offer parents a collective forum, has met with refusal from the Secretary of State (Spencer, 1990). It does not look as though the commitment to parental choice is a commitment to parental power.

If the tests will not automatically work in the interests of parents, whose interests do they serve? It is worth noting that recent history shows the debate over assessments to have been revitalised around the notion of 'standards' in the mid 1970s, after a relatively short period during which continuous assessment by teachers had gained some acceptance in the 16+ CSE examinations and was making small inroads into the more respectable and higher status GCE. The debate, while often used to voice concern over the standard of work of school leavers ('outputs'), is also broad enough to take in teaching methods and learning processes. Most recently it has hit the media as a 'real books' versus 'phonics' controversy over methods of teaching children to read.

Crude numerical ranking of standard assessments would provide management with league tables of schools and teachers, and allow them to compute measurable costs against measurable results; to compare the presumed relative efficiency of one against another.

However, the other assumption, that the figures can be used to raise standards through open access and competition, is quite different and, in the light of the argument that neighbourhood catchments are more likely to be reflected in results than anything else, somewhat ingenuous. Implicit in the model is the assumption that connections can be made quite directly between test results and the way teachers work to achieve them. This information cannot be read from the figures, only implied. Somehow (unspecified) teachers are supposed to gain from being associated with a pattern of good results and hence be motivated to teach children even better.

Paradoxically, teachers who find they are staffing a school (or teaching a class) which is generating a pattern of below average results are also supposed to be motivated to teach better. Otherwise, the theory goes, they will face falling rolls, because parents (on behalf of their children) will vote with their feet. Again we have here a managerial interest in assessment, should the results be regarded as crucial information for school management teams in developing their plans and targeting their efforts for improvement and staff development.

Yet, the information required to improve teaching processes, is useless if it is presented as a matter of league tables. Even assuming reliable and valid results, league tables of crude quantities would still offer little or no indication of how the situation might be remedied. In order to plan to remedy defects, even on an individualistic, deficit model, management teams must have information which helps them to diagnose where exactly each child or teacher or class is having problems. Perhaps there is a belief somewhere that test results really will identify good and bad teachers, and effective and ineffective methods, in simple, readily interpretable dichotomies which present obvious solutions for management action.

A third possibility is that assessment would mark any particular pupil's individual achievement of a short-term goal. Such goals might be part of a negotiated programme of work, or derived from a set of criteria for achievement established by the tests. The problem with negotiation is that teachers can underestimate or overestimate their pupils' abilities, given the power differential in the negotiations, and hence have expectations that are too low or too high. The results would be individualised and useless as guides to policy. On the other hand, if teachers are concerned for criterion referenced results, they will teach to the test. To ensure a broad curriculum, criteria would be required to cover every possible detail and schooling would become a tedious series of mechanistic competency tests. All that managers would discover would be whether or not children could perform to order.

A fourth possibility would not use testing for policy making at all, but would confine it to teaching–learning situations where research had illustrated its appropriateness. Instead of looking for standardised assessment results, management might concentrate the school's development policy more on strategic issues aimed at enabling teachers to develop their professional expertise collectively in a supportive community of parents and pupils. However, this would be a devolved, rather than a delegated form of local management and this is not the place to develop this scenario, simply to acknowledge it as a possibility.

On the evidence so far, the purposes of instituting national assessments at 7, 11, 14 and 16, are unclear, but appear much more likely to be geared to organisational objectives than parental choice; to be centred as much on processes of management control as on processes of education. More light may be thrown on the subject by widening the debate and examining further some of the confusions which surround the whole notion of assessment.

Assessment in Crisis?

Confusion over the purposes of schooling and assessment; between assessments which normatively grade pupils' achievements, individually diagnose pupils' difficulties or set objectives and assess pupils' work against specified criteria of achievement, is becoming a major issue as the evidence grows that the managerial and the contemporary educational approaches to schooling exhibit different priorities and inhabit different worlds of meaning.

Bates (1984, 1987, 1988a, 1988b) identified conflicts in the field of pupil testing where procedures geared to standardising, classifying and ranking 'outputs', fitted uneasily into a teaching context best served by testing for the diagnosis and treatment of individual difficulties (Bates, 1984).

Broadfoot (1988: 5) saw the problem as the persistence of:

The long standing pre-eminence of psychometric concerns about accurate comparative measurement of both student potential and student achievement (which) has only been matched by the associated concern with selection, prediction and accountability'.

Broadfoot sets these 'mechanistic' concerns against the 'student centred', 'educationist' approach which, she argues, is geared to each individual pupil's needs. In an educationist context, pupils are encouraged to set their own goals, review their own progress and work with teachers in a joint endeavour. In other words, pupils are encouraged to manage themselves — self motivation and self-management of work with negotiated and agreed objectives, rather than experience the imposition of a predefined course which takes no account of the individual pupil. However, such a process would provide nothing standardised to guide management strategists who want a simple measure of how schools, in general, are doing.

Murphy's comment on the original proposals from the Task Group on Assessment and Testing (TGAT), set up by the Secretary of State in 1987 to advise him on testing processes in the 1988 Education Reform Act, points to the compromise that eventually emerged. He claimed they were 'a kind of half-way house between conventional externally devised written tests and coursework undertaken by teachers' (Murphy, 1990: 44). Murphy (1990: 44) sees this as 'a Houdini-like act of escaping from an impossible situation'.

Since then we have seen the consequences of this attempt at a theoretical compromise reverberate into schools as teacher overload. Experiences at the piloting of the new standard assessment tasks (SATs) and the subsequent reduction in their number has not altered the fundamental issue. The goals of the national assessment programme remain confused rather than common (St John Brooks, 1990).

This mix of approaches — coexisting in an uneasy compromise whereby pupils are exhorted to engage in self-managed, student centred, wide ranging, criterion-referenced learning for formative, continuous and diagnostic and even self-assessment (as in profiling), only to have their individual achievements reduced to simplistic, standardised, norm-referenced grades as and when required for impersonal, external consumption — is not confined to the new proposals for standard national assessments.

Corroborative case study evidence is available from an examination of teachers of English in a comprehensive school implementing GCSE. In a scheme involving continuous assessment, broadly under the control of schools stretching across four counties, teachers were found to be experiencing a variety of powerful, conflicting pressures as they attempted to motivate pupils by continuous assessment over a two year period which culminated in the standardised GCSE grades. Some resorted to a strategy of maintaining the lower achieving pupils' hope of a worthwhile result by avoiding telling them the 'real' grade equivalents of their coursework, for fear they would see early on that the end result would not be worth having. Yet throughout the period, it was the processes geared to the ultimate grading which dominated (Taylor & Wallace, 1990).

I have spent some time on this overview of the paradoxes in assessment, because local management is the linchpin of the wheel of (differentially) funded 'curriculum entitlement'. Around LMS, both age-weighted funding and each individual pupil's 'entitlement' revolve. Standard assessment becomes the mechanism for measuring the extent to which pupils have received their funded 'entitlement'. However, at the point where the 'system' is geared to judging schooling outcomes, the information required centrally for measuring standardised assessment objectives does not match well with those alternative educational objectives which are aimed at encouraging pupil–teacher co-operation over the 'self-management' of pupils' educational progress. Even if they did, the funding process is geared to neither. Entitlement is not best measured by a test, although it might be funded by one! The linchpin fails to connect. Yet new myths are being packaged to obscure the lack of logic in the system, string the different bits together, and create an image of 'balance'. In the process, LMS challenges the language and practices of the human qualities in education in favour of mechanistically derived quantities.

LMS and the Language Game

Take first the concept of value. Attempts to argue philosophically the case for 'educational values' are already being cut across by the commercial concept of 'value for money'; a concept which obscures questions about who is making judgements about which values, and even who is paying for what kind of 'value for money'.

Similarly, 'evaluation' has tended to lose its traditional associations with continuing moral judgements to absorb the meaning given to an audit of outcomes set against predefined behavioural (or financial) objectives. Taken as a numerical or financial, rather than an educational evaluation, it is a small step before pupil–teacher relationships begin to be measured by a cost-benefit analysis of success and failure which turns 'accountability' into a measure of financial costs against the measurable results. The implications of these changes are well-illustrated by another potential import from the world of commercial management: the redefinition of 'quality' to accommodate the requirements of the new 'quality managers':

> The first absolute of quality management defines quality. Typically, quality is viewed as goodness, elegance, value, or meeting customer requirements. Unfortunately, the perception of goodness and value is subjective. As such, the management of value is a personal thing, and is not easily communicated and managed. To avoid this subjective understanding, quality is defined as conformity to requirements. (Hutton, 1990: 290)

Hutton goes on to argue that quality is evident when the product conforms to requirements, and, 'quality is measured by the money it costs to do things wrong' (Hutton, 1990: 291). Thus, in one bound, quality becomes quantity. (See also Mortimore & Stone, 1991)

Another effect of this slippage from an educational concept to a numerical one is to turn the concept of self-management on its head. Instead of the community of teachers, pupils, parents and governors self-managing their schools, they are forced by the strait-jacket supplied by the legislation on funding, curriculum and assessment to manage their schools within a perverse and contradictory system.

Some Food for Thought

The evidence in this book is necessarily limited and it is early days to establish a pattern of practice under LMS. Nevertheless, representing a wide range of experience and interests, the authors evoke a sense that LMS is not the panacea it was supposed to be. Further evidence of the consequence of these structural problems, this time from Northern Ireland, where financial delegation was introduced into nine schools in 1988, and extended to 56 in 1989, comes from the NI Council for Educational Research who have some preliminary results from a study of the pilot schools. Among a number of significant findings from the questionnaires and interviews, were echoes of the concerns and developments indicated in this book. These included anxieties over funding and the search for financial and administrative experts to help; the dominance of financial issues on governors' committee agendas, in spite of expressed commitment to curricula-led policies; difficulties associated with planning ahead in an unpredictable environment; shortage of time to cope with existing problems, let alone plan ahead, and shortage of advice about what was wanted; a 'distancing' of principals (heads) from curricula matters by the changed nature of their workloads; an interest by senior teachers in working on policy-making committees; and a belief that there was little purpose in involving parents 'more closely in school affairs'. The dominant role on governing bodies and subcommittees was that of the head. The development plans which existed had been drawn up by the principal teachers of fewer than half the schools. Although laid down as a 'requirement' to be met by governing boards, teachers and governors were 'not yet familiar' with the document giving guidelines on what was wanted (Wells & McKibben, 1990a, 1990b, 1990c). In the managerial/educational battle, the heads had again attempted to contain the damage rather as Bowe & Ball, and Broadbent *et al.* observed in their studies earlier in this volume.

Conclusion

In conclusion, I shall group together a small selection of assumed equivalences, drawing on the earlier papers in this book, to highlight the current confusion. On the one hand lie the educational processes, on the other, the commercial managerial. In combination they cohabit in a most uneasy 'balance':

(1) Curriculum entitlement and complex patterns of individual pupil's needs are assumed to be met from formula funding largely based on age-weighted numbers; LEAs vary in the way they have calculated the weightings and the funds they apply to them (Stewart, Maden, Lee).

(2) Delegated powers of management are supposed to devolve both power and accountability on to schools, but the powers are small in effect and are more than countered by a massive increase in workload associated with accountability. This currently devolves onto a small management group or team who may operate a technocratic, hierarchical system of control in the name of local management (McGovern, Bowe & Ball, Broadbent et al., Levačić).

(3) Numbers-driven management substitutes for issue-driven management and financial viability substitutes for educational viability (Broadbent et al., Keep).

(4) A delivered curriculum substitutes for a professionally developed curriculum (McBride). However, the process may not be a simple one of de-professionalism. Professionals are institutionalised into the new system as changes occur but, once drawn into collective processes of decision making, find creative ways of using what is 'delivered' to develop their professional practice (McBride, Busher).

(5) Governing boards, although set up to manage on behalf of parents, may consist of individuals who have little or no contact with, or knowledge of, the parents, teachers and pupils they supposedly represent (Leask, Broadbent et al.).

Looking ahead, it seems likely that parental choice of schools and open access may well operate as a licence to heads and governors to exclude pupils whose presence will depress a school's overall results or increase the costs too much. Under a voucher system, choice becomes synonymous with ability to pay more by 'topping up' and LMS marks a significant step in that direction. The consequences for those who will have no choice have yet to be properly ascertained. Such consequences will no doubt be mitigated in a variety of ways by teachers' professional practices, but they will not be an effect of consumer choice. LMS is an act of political policy.

References

AINLEY, P. 1990, *Training Turns to Enterprise: Vocational Education in the Marketplace*. London: Tufnell Press.

ALDER, M. and RAAB, G. 1988, Exit, choice and loyalty: The impact of parental choice on admission to school in Edinburgh and Dundee. *Journal of Educational Policy* 3, 2.

ALLEN, D. 1985, Strategic management accounting. *Management Accounting* March.

ARMSTRONG, P. 1989, Limits and possibilities for HRM in an age of management accountancy. In J. STOREY (ed.) *New Perspectives on Human Resource Management* (pp. 154–66). London: Routledge.

Audit Commission 1988, Occasional Paper No 5: Delegation of Management Authority to Schools. London: HMSO.

— 1989a, *Assuring Quality in Education: The Role of Local Education Authority Inspectors and Advisers*. London: HMSO.

— 1989b, Occasional Paper No. 10: Losing an Empire, Finding a Role: The LEA of the Future. London: HMSO.

BALL, S. J. 1990, *Politics and Policy-making in Education: Explorations in Policy Sociology*. London: Routledge.

BALL, S. J. and BOWE, R. 1990, The micropolitics of radical change: Budgets, management and control in British schools. Paper delivered to the American Research Association Conference, Boston.

BARNES, J. and LUCAS, H. 1974. Positive discrimination in education: Individuals, groups and institutions. In T. LEGGATT (ed.) *Sociological Theory and Survey Research*. London: Sage.

BATES, RICHARD J. 1984, Educational versus managerial evaluation in schools. In P. BROADFOOT (ed.) *Selection, Certification and Control*. London and Philadelphia: Falmer.

— 1987, Corporate culture, schooling and educational administration. *Educational Administration Quarterly* 4, 79–115.

— 1988a, Administrative theory and the social construction of schools. *Discourse* 2, 111–26.

— 1988b, Is there a new paradigm in educational administration? Paper presented to the Organisational Theory Special Interest Group Annual Conference of the American Educational Research Association. New Orleans, 5th–10th April.

BARTLETT, T. (1989) Within the LEA: A collaborative model for INSET. In R. MCBRIDE (ed.) *The In-service Training of Teachers: Some Issues and Perspectives*. Lewes: Falmer Press.

BAUER, A. (ed.) 1966, *Social Indicators*. London: MIT Press.

BAUMBER, A. 1990, LMS and related issues. Association of Educational Psychologists, AEP/58/90 (mimeo).

BEVAN, G. 1989, Reforming UK health care: Internal markets or emergent planning? *Fiscal Studies* 10, 1, 53–71.

BLACKBURN, L. 1990, Competition prompts heads to consider code of conduct. *Times Educational Supplement* 1st June. London: Times Newspapers.

BOWE, R. and BALL, S. J. 1990, Managing change in the educational market. *The Journal of the Centre for the Study of Comprehensive Schools* 2, 2, spring.

— (forthcoming) Subject to change? Subject departments and the 'implementation' of national curriculum policy: an overview of the issues. *Journal of Curriculum Studies*.

BRIGHOUSE, T. 1988a, Playing the game by Rawls' rules. *Times Educational Supplement* 1st January, 1990. London: Times Newspapers.

— 1988b, Targets for Mr Baker. *Times Educational Supplement* 16th September. London: Times Newspapers.

BROADBENT, J. 1991, A 'middle range approach' for understanding accounting in organisations: A model and its application in case study in the NHS. Discussion Paper, University of Sheffield.

BROADBENT, J., LAUGHLIN, R. C. and READ, S. 1991, Recent financial and administrative changes in the NHS: A critical theory analysis. *Critical Perspectives in Accounting* 2, 1–29.

BROADFOOT, P. M. 1988, The national assessment framework and records of achievement. In H. TORRANCE (ed.) *National Assessment and Testing: A Research Response*. Cumbria: British Educational Research Association.

BROOKE, M. Z. 1986, *International Management: A Review of Strategies and Options*. London: Hutchinson.

BROWN, D. J. 1990, *Decentralisation and School Based Management*. London and Basingstoke: Falmer Press.

BUSH, T. 1990, Going it alone: Managing grant-maintained schools. *Educational Management and Administration* 18, 4.

BUSHER, H. 1989, Bringing out a new publication — the role of a catalyst in the micropolitics of the management of change in education. *British Educational Research Journal* 15, 1, 77–87.

CABLE, J. R. 1988, Organisational form and economic performance. In STEVE THOMPSON and MIKE WRIGHT (eds) *Internal Organisation, Efficiency and Profit*. Oxford: Philip Allan.

CALDWELL, B. 1990, School based decision-making. In J. CHAPMAN (ed.) *School Based Decision-making and Management*. London and Basingstoke: Falmer Press.

CALDWELL, B. J. and SPINKS, J. M. 1988, *The Self-Managing School*. Lewes: Falmer Press.

Cambridgeshire Education Committee 1990, Local Management — the next phase of development. Chief Education Officer's Proposals 4th December. Cambridge LEA (mimeo).

CANE, B. 1969, *In-Service Training: A Study of Teachers' Views and Preferences*. Slough: NFER.

CHAMBERS, D. 1988, Learning from markets. *Public Money and Management*. Winter, 47–50.

CLEGG, H. 1964, Employers' Associations: Should they be abolished? *Federation News* February. London: EEF.

COASE, R. H. 1937, The nature of the firm. *Economica* (new series) 4, 386–405.

COLLINSON, D. 1988, *Barriers to Fair Selection: A Multi-sector Study of Recruitment Practices.* London: HMSO.

CONWAY, J. A. 1978, Power and participatory decision-making in selected English schools. *Journal of Educational Administration* 16, 1, 80–96.

Coopers and Lybrand Associates 1988, Local Management of Schools. Report to the DES. London: HMSO.

CYERT, R. M. and MARCH, J. G. 1963, *A Behavioural Study of the Firm.* Englewood Cliffs: Prentice-Hall.

DAY, C. 1985, *Managing Primary Schools.* London: Harper and Rowe.

DEEM, R. and BREHONY, K. 1990, The long and the short of it. *Times Educational Supplement* 13th July, 10. London: Times Newspapers.

DES (Department of Education and Science) 1972, *Teacher Education and Training* (The James Report). London: HMSO.

— 1978a, Making INSET work, in-service education and training for teachers: A basis for discussion. London: HMSO.

— 1978b, *Special Educational Needs* (The Warnock Report). London: HMSO.

— 1983, Circular 3/83. London: HMSO.

— 1986, Circular 6/86. London: HMSO.

— 1987a, Education (training grants) regulations. London: HMSO.

— 1987b, *Education Reform: The Government's Proposals for Schools.* London: HMSO.

— 1987c, *Teachers' Pay and Conditions Act.* London: HMSO.

— 1988a, Circular 7/88, Education Reform Act: Local Management of Schools. London: HMSO.

— 1988b, Press Release No. 249/1988. London: DES.

— 1989, Circular 22/89, Assessments and statements of special educational needs: Procedures within the education, health and social services. London: HMSO.

— 1990a, John MacGregor publishes school budget figures. *DES News* 310/90, 1st October. London: DES.

— 1990b, Local management of schools: Further guidance, Regulations issued on 11th December. London: HMSO.

— 1991, Local Management of Schools: Further guidance, Regulations issued on 22 April. London: HMSO.

DES/HMI 1991, *Governing Bodies Now.* London: HMSO.

DONOUGHUE, C., BALL, S., GLAISTER, B. and HAND, G. (eds) 1981, *In-service: The Teacher and the School.* London: Kogan Page/Open University Press.

DUFFY, M. 1990, Heresy and Magic. *Times Educational Supplement* LMS Guide, Part 1, 16th February. London: Times Newspapers.

Edmonton Public Schools 1989, Governance and operations: Consulting services pilot project. June, Edmonton: Canada.

— 1990, Consulting Services. Edmonton: Canada.

Education 1990a, MacGregor urges self-determination to end the LEA 'empire'. 13th April, Vol. 175, No. 15, 361–2.

— 1990b, Uncertainty blights community education. 18th May, 175, 20, 485.

Education (No. 2) Act 1986, c. 61. London: HMSO.

Education Reform Act 1988, c. 40. London: HMSO.

EDWARDS, J. 1985, Social indicators and the concept of the quality of life. In A. ROBERTSON and A. OSBORNE (eds) *Planning to Care.* Aldershot: Gower.

ENTHOVEN, A. J. 1978, Consumer health choice plan. *New England Journal of Medicine* 28, 650–8 and 709–20.

— 1988, *Theory and Practice of Managed Competition in Health Care Finance*. Amsterdam: North-Holland.

ERAUT, M. 1988, Management knowledge: Its nature and its development. In J. CALDERHEAD (ed.) *Teachers' Professional Learning*. Lewes: Falmer Press.

EVANS, J. and LUNI, I. 1990, *Local Management of Schools and Special Educational Needs*. London: Institute of Education.

EVERARD, K. B. 1986, *Developing Management in Schools*. Oxford and New York: Basil Blackwell.

FERNER, A. 1988, *Governments, Managers and Industrial Relations — Public Enterprises and their Political Environments*. Oxford and New York: Basil Blackwell.

FLANDERS, A. 1974, The tradition of voluntarism. *British Journal of Industrial Relations* 12, 352–70.

FLUDE, M. and HAMMER, M. (eds) 1990, *The Education Reform Act*. London: Falmer Press.

FRIEDMAN, M. and FRIEDMAN, R. 1980, *Free to Choose: A Personal Statement*. London: Secker and Warburg.

GIBBS, C. 1990, Improving home/school communication. Unpublished MA dissertation, Open University.

GODDARD, D. 1985, ACSET: Its implementation in a wider context. *School Organisation* 5, 3, 235–45.

GOODCHILD, S. and HOLLY, P. 1989, *Management for Change: The Garth Hill Experience*. Lewes: Falmer Press.

GOOLD, M. and CAMPBELL, A. 1986, *Strategies and Styles: The Role of the Centre in Managing Diversified Corporations*. Oxford and New York: Basil Blackwell.

GOSPEL, H. F. 1973, An approach to a theory of the firm in industrial relations. *British Journal of Industrial Relations* July, 11, 211–29.

GRUNDY, S. 1990, Beyond professionalism. In W. CARR (ed.) *Quality in Teaching*. Lewes: Falmer Press.

HARGREAVES, D. H. and HOPKINS, D. 1991, *School Development Planning*. London: Cassell.

HARGREAVES, D. H., HOPKINS, D. and LEASK, M. 1989a, Planning for school development: A note from the project team to Local Education Authorities. London, DES, August (mimeo).

— 1989b, Planning for school development: Advice to governors and head teachers. London: DES, December.

— 1990, The management of development planning: A paper for Local Education Authorities. London, DES, April (mimeo).

HARLAND, J. 1987, The new INSET: A transformation scene. In R. MURPHY and H. TORRANCE (eds) *Evaluating Education: Issues and Methods*. London: Harper and Rowe.

HARVEY, D. 1990, *The Condition of Postmodernity: An Enquiry into the Origins of Social Change*. Oxford and New York: Basil Blackwell.

HAYEK, F. A. von, 1960, *The Constitution of Liberty*. London: RKP.

— 1976, *Law, Legislation and Liberty, Vol. 2, Rules and Order*. London: RKP.

— 1989, Spontaneous order and organised order. In N. MOLDOVSKY (ed.) *Order — With or Without Design*. London: Centre for Research into Communist Economies.

HEMMINGS, S. 1990, Determined to see it through. *Times Educational Supplement* 20th July, 16. London: Times Newspapers.

HEMMINGS, S., DEEM, R. and BREHONY, K. 1990, Governors working with schools —
    towards a new partnership? Paper delivered to the British Educational Research
    Association, Annual Conference, Roehampton Institute, 1st September.
HOLT, M. 1987, Bureaucracy benefits. *Times Educational Supplement* 18th September.
HORN, J. 1987, Diving into dangerous waters. *Times Educational Supplement* 18th
    December.
HOYLE, E. 1983, The professionalisation of teachers: A paradox. In *Is Teaching a
    Profession?* Bedford Way Paper No. 15. London: Institute of Education.
HUGHILL, B. 1989, Factory whistle drowns out school bell. *Times Educational
    Supplement* 8th September.
HUTTON, M. 1990, Competing in the 21st century. In G. K. KANJI (ed.) *Total Quality
    Management* 1, 3, 289–92.
ILEA (Inner London Education Authority) 1982. Educational priority indices — a
    new perspective. Research and Statistics Report, No. 858/82. London: ILEA.
— 1985, *Improving Primary Schools* (The Thomas Report). London: ILEA.
— 1988, *Secondary School Development Plans*. London: ILEA.
JOHNSON, H. T. and KAPLAN, R. S. 1987, *Relevance Lost*. Cambridge, Mass.: Harvard
    Business School Press.
JONES, K., O'SULLIVAN, F. and REID, K. 1987, The challenge of the new INSET.
    Educational Review 39, 3, 191–202.
KEAT, R. and ABERCROMBIE, N. 1991, *Enterprise Culture*. London: Routledge.
KEEP, E. 1989, Corporate training strategies: The vital component? In J. STOREY (ed.)
    New Perspectives on Human Resource Management (pp. 109–25). London:
    Routledge.
— 1990, Do borrowed clothes fit? Some question marks concerning the importation of
    private sector management and market models into secondary education.
    University of Warwick, Industrial Relations Research Unit, (mimeo).
LAUGHLIN, R. C. 1987, Accounting systems in organisational contexts: A case for
    critical theory. *Accounting, Organisations and Society* 12, 5, 479–502.
— 1990, Field study in accounting: A case for middle range thinking. Paper delivered to
    the Adelaide Accounting Research Meeting, 12th July 1990.
— 1991 Environmental disturbances and organizational transitions and trans-
    formations: Some alternative models. *Organization Studies* 12(2), 209–32.
LEE, T. 1990a, Formula funding and social disadvantage: Summary of LEA methods.
    Bath: Centre for the Analysis of Social Policy (mimeo).
— 1990b, Special educational needs and social disadvantage under LMS: Present
    issues and future implications. *ACE Bulletin*, 35, May–June. London, Advisory
    Centre for Education.
— 1990c, Carving out the cash for schools: LMS and the new ERA of education.
    Social Policy Paper 17, Bath: Centre for the Analysis of Social Policy.
LODGE, B. 1989, Shower of gifts entices parents. *Times Educational Supplement* 3
    November.
London Borough of Enfield 1985, Supporting institutional development: Curriculum
    initiatives Group. London Borough of Enfield, October, (mimeo).
LYONS, G. 1976, *Heads' Tasks*. Slough: NFER.
MACINTYRE, A. 1981, *After Virtue*. London: Duckworth.
MADEN, M. 1989, New networks for old. *Times Educational Supplement* 1st September.
    London: Times Newspapers.
MAKINS, V. 1990, A united front. *Times Educational Supplement* 18th May. London:
    Times Newspapers.

MARGINSON, P., EDWARDS, P., MARTIN, R., PURCELL, J. and SISSON, K. 1988, *Beyond the Workplace*. Oxford and New York: Basil Blackwell.

MCBRIDE, R. 1989, (ed.) *The In-Service Training of Teachers: Some Issues and Perspectives*. Lewes: Falmer Press.

MCKINSEY & CO. INC. 1988, *Strengthening Competitiveness in the UK Electronics Industry*. London: NEDO.

MCMAHON, A., BOLAM, R., ABBOTT, T. and HOLLY, P. 1984, *Guidelines for the Review and Internal Development in Schools: Secondary School Handbook*. Harlow: Longman.

MINTZBERG 1979, *The Structuring of Organisations: A Synthesis of the Research*. Englewood Cliffs, NJ: Prentice Hall.

MORTIMORE, P. and STONE, E. C. 1991, Measuring educational quality. *British Journal of Educational Studies* 39, 1, 69–82.

MULLEN, P. 1990, Which internal market? The NHS White Paper and internal markets. *Financial Accountability and Management* 6, 1, 33–50.

MURPHY, R. 1990, National assessment proposals: Analysing the debate. In M. FLUDE and M. HAMMER *The Education Reform Act — 1988* (pp. 37–49). Basingstoke: Falmer Press.

NASH, I. 1989, Image-makers of the sixth. *Times Educational Supplement*, 5th May. London: Times Newspapers.

— 1990, Parents puzzled by 'consumers' of education tag. *Times Educational Supplement* 13th July, 10. London, Times Newspapers.

NEEDHAM, B. and WILLIAMS, T. 1989, *Analysis of Local Management of Schools Formulae*. Slough: Education Management Information Exchange, NFER.

NEILSON, R. P., PETERS, M. and HISRICH, R. 1985, Intrapreneurship strategy for internal markets — corporate, non-profit and governmental institution cases. *Strategic Management Journal* 6, 181–9.

NEWSAM, P. 1989, Life in the fast lane. *Times Educational Supplement* 29th December. London: Times Newspapers.

O'CONNOR, M. 1989, Rock of Ages Cleft for LEAs, *The Guardian* 10th October 1990, 25 London and Manchester: Guardian Newspapers.

OLSON, M. 1971, *The Logic of Collective Action — Public Goods and the Theory of Groups*. Cambridge, Mass.: Harvard University Press.

PAISEY, A. 1981, *Organisation and Management in School*. Harlow: Longman.

PERKIN, H. 1989, *The Rise of the Professional Society: England Since 1880*. London: Routledge.

Plowden Report 1967, Children and their primary schools — Report of the Central Advisory Council for Education. London: HMSO.

POSTER, C. and DAY, C. (eds) 1988, *Partnership in Education Management*. London: Routledge.

POWER, M. and LAUGHLIN, R. C. 1990, From steering to colonisation: Accounting and critical theory. Paper delivered to the Critical Theory and Management Studies Conference, Shrewsbury, April.

PRAHALAD, C. K. and HAMEL, G. 1990, The core competence of the corporation. *Harvard Business Review* May/June, 79–91.

PURCELL, J. 1989, The impact of corporate strategy on human resource management. In J. STOREY (ed.) *New Perspectives on Human Resource Management* (pp. 67–91). London: Routledge.

PYKE, N. 1990, Cuts blamed for rise in special needs referrals. *Times Educational Supplement*, 21st September. London: Times Newspapers.

RICHARDS, S. 1987. The financial management initiative. In: J. GRETTON and A. HARRISON (eds) *Reshaping Central Government*. London: Policy Journals.

RICHARDSON, G. B. 1972, The organisation of industry. *The Economic Journal* September, 883–96.

RUTTER, M., MAUGHAN, B., MORTIMORE, P. and OUSTON, J. 1979, *Fifteen Thousand Hours: Secondary Schools and their Effects on Children*. Shepton Mallet: Open Books.

ST JOHN BROOKS, C. 1990, National curriculum update. *Times Educational Supplement* 14th September, 10. London: Times Newspapers.

SAUNDERS, M. 1986, Perceptions on TRIST: Implications for INSET. *Research Papers in Education* 2, 2, 106–12. Slough: NFER.

SCHON, D. 1983, *The Reflective Practitioner*. Aldershot, Hants: M. Temple-Smith.

School Management Task Force 1990, *Developing School Management: The Way Forward*. London: HMSO.

SEXTON, S. 1990, Free market's better values. *Education Guardian* 14th August. London and Manchester: Guardian Newspapers.

SHONFIELD, A. and SHAW, S. 1972, *Social Indicators and Social Policy*. London: Heinemann Educational Books.

SIMON, H. A. 1959, Theories of decision-making in economics and behavioural science. *American Economic Review* 69, 3, June, 253–81.

SIMONS, H., ELLIOTT, J. and MACDONALD, B. 1988, Kettering alternative approach: independent external validation. Northamptonshire County Council (mimeo).

SISSON, K. 1989a, Personnel management in perspective. In K. SISSON (ed.) *Personnel Management in Britain* (pp. 3–21). Oxford and New York: Basil Blackwell.

— (1989b) Personnel management in transition? In K. SISSON (ed.) *Personnel Management in Britain* (pp. 23–52). Oxford and New York: Basil Blackwell.

— 1990, Introducing the *Human Resource Management Journal. Human Resource Management Journal* 1, 1, Autumn, 1–11.

SMALLEY, T. (1989) Regional and sub-regional co-ordination of INSET. In R. MCBRIDE (ed.) *In-Service Training of Teachers: Some Issues and Perspectives.* Lewes: Falmer Press.

SMILANICH, B. 1988, Devolution in Edmonton Public Schools: Ten years later. *Edmonton Public Schools*. Edmonton, Canada (mimeo).

SMITH, D. and TOMLINSON, S. 1989, *The School Effect: A Study of Multi-Racial Comprehensives.* London: Policy Studies Institute.

SPENCER, D. 1990, Parent–teacher group beset by new discord. *Times Educational Supplement* 9th June, A3. London: Times Newspapers.

STENHOUSE, L. 1975, *An Introduction to Curriculum Research and Development*. London: Heinemann.

STERNE, M. 1987, Loose thinking. *Times Educational Supplement* 27th November. London: Times Newspapers.

STEWART, J. and RANSON, S. 1988, Management in the public domain. *Public Money and Management* Spring/Summer, 13–19.

STOREY, J. 1989, Introduction: From personnel management to human resource management. In J. STOREY (ed.) *New Perspectives on Human Resource Management* (pp. 1–18). London: Routledge.

STREECK, W. 1989, Skills and the limits of neo-liberalism: The enterprise of the future as a place of learning. *Work, Employment and Society* 3, 1, 89–104.

SUTCLIFFE, J. 1989, Another heavy burden or the answer to all ailments? *Times Educational Supplement* September. London: Times Newspapers.

TAYLOR, J. and WALLACE, G. 1990, Some dilemmas in implementing the criteria for GCSE English. *British Journal of Sociology of Education* 11, 1, 49–64.

THOMAS, G. 1990, *Setting up LMS: A Study of Local Education Authorities' Submissions to the DES*. Milton Keynes: Open University Learning Materials Office.

THOMAS, H. 1988, Pupils as vouchers. *Times Educational Supplement* 2nd December. London: Times Newspapers.

THOMPSON, Q. 1990, Is LMS still on track? *Times Educational Supplement* 6th June. London: Times Newspapers.

TIMPERLEY, S. and SISSON, K. 1989, From manpower planning to human resource planning? In K. SISSON (ed.) *Personnel Management in Britain* (pp. 103–24). Oxford and New York: Basil Blackwell.

TORRINGTON, D. and WEIGHTMAN, J. 1983 Why heads should not be seen as managing directors. *Times Educational Supplement* 9th December. London: Times Newspapers.

WATSON, L. 1969, Office and expertise in the secondary school. *Educational Research* 11, 104–12.

WEBER, M. (1960) In R. BENDIX (ed.) *Max Weber, An Intellectual Portrait*. London: Methuen.

WELLS, I. and McKIBBEN, T. 1990a, *First Experiences of LMS: Summary Series No. 12*. Belfast: Northern Ireland Council for Educational Research.

— 1990b, *Local Management of Schools: Questionnaire Evidence from the Pilot School*. Belfast: Northern Ireland Council for Educational Research.

— 1990c, *Local Management of Schools: Information from Interviews with Teachers and School Governors*. Belfast: Northern Ireland Council for Educational Research.

White Paper (Cmnd. 8616) 1982, *Efficiency and Effectiveness in the Civil Service*. London: HMSO.

WIDEEN, M. and ANDREWS, I. 1987. (eds) *Staff Development for School Improvement*. Lewes: Falmer Press.

WILKINSON, C. and CAVE, E. 1988, *Teaching and Managing: Inseparable Activities in Schools*. London: Croom Helm.

WILLIAMSON, O. E. 1975, *Markets and Hierarchies: Analysis and Antitrust Implications*. New York: Free Press.

— 1985, *The Economic Institutions of Capitalism: Firms, Markets and Relational Contracting*. New York: Free Press.

WOOTTON, J. 1989, For LMS read one 'ell of a Mess. *The Guardian*, 20th May 1990. London and Manchester: Guardian Newspapers.

WRIGHT, D. 1987, Is teaching still a profession? The case of GCSE INSET. *British Journal of In-Service* 13, 102–05.

Notes on Contributors

Stephen J. Ball is Professor of Education in the Centre for Educational Studies, King's College, University of London, where he has worked since 1985. He is a sociologist and ethnographer and his interests are focused upon the formation and implementation of education policy, the sociology of education and ethnographic methods. He is author of *Beachside Comprehensive* (Cambridge 1981), *Education-Sociology in Focus* (Longman, 1985), *The Micropolitics of the School* (Routledge, 1987) and *Education Politics and Policy Making* (Routledge, 1990), as well as editor of several collections, most recently *Foucault and Education* (Routledge, 1990). He is managing editor of the *Journal of Education Policy*.

Richard Bowe is a Research Fellow at King's College, University of London. He is currently working on a project funded by ESRC, looking at the impact of the educational market (proposed in the 1988 Education Reform Act) upon schools and local authorities.

Jane Broadbent qualified as an accountant before returning to full-time education, graduating from the University of York with a BA in Sociology. Subsequently she obtained an MA in Accounting and Financial Management from the University of Sheffield, where she is now a Lecturer in the Management School. Her research interests are focused on accounting in the public sector, particularly in the fields of Education and Health.

Hugh Busher is a Lecturer in Education at Loughborough University. After teaching in comprehensive schools for many years, he now focuses on their politics and management and on the relationships between people which these activities engender.

Nigel Dandy graduated from Sheffield University with a BA in Accounting and Financial Management. He then joined the teaching staff as a Lecturer in Accounting, with teaching interests which included the use of different methodological approaches in the study of accounting, and the analysis of managerial situations using case studies. He is currently pursuing an M.Phil. degree, researching the history of state funding of education before the 1988 Reform Act, and is involved with other members of the department in studying the introduction of LMS.

Ewart Keep is a Research Fellow in the Industrial Relations Research Unit at Warwick Business School. He graduated in Modern History and Politics from Royal Holloway College, London, in 1979, and worked for three years in the CBI's Education and Training Directorate. His research at the IRRU has covered UK training policy, and is currently focused on strategic personnel management policies for the secondary school teaching workforce.

Richard Laughlin is Professor of Accounting in the Sheffield University Management School. He worked as a trainee and manager in a professional accounting practice and as a consultant accountant before joining the University of Sheffield as a Lecturer in Accounting and Financial Management. He has been lecturing at Sheffield since 1973 apart from a two year spell (1976–8) when he worked as a consultant in the Church of England. He has a Master of Social Science degree (M.Soc.Sc.) from Birmingham and a Ph.D. from Sheffield as well as being a Chartered Accountant. He has a wide range of publications in academic as well as professional journals, books and conference proceedings, many of which develop an understanding of the way accounting and finance practices relate to, and change with, their social and political organisational contexts.

Marilyn Leask was Research Associate to the DES funded School Development Plans Project which produced advice for heads, teachers and governors on planning for school development. She is now a Senior Lecturer in Education at Bedford College of Higher Education. Her interests lie primarily in the areas of evaluation and assessment, science education and school management and governance. She is co-author of *The Search for Quality* (Paul Chapman, in press).

Tim Lee is a Research Fellow at the Centre for Analysis of Social Policy, University of Bath. His current research on LMS is funded by the ESRC and entitled 'Social Disadvantage and LEA Resource Allocation to Schools'. Prior to this research he was Lecturer in Social Policy at Bath.

Rosalind Levačić is Senior Lecturer in Educational Policy and Management at the Open University, having previously lectured in economics. She has written a number of articles on local management of schools and is editor of *Financial Management in Education (1989)* (Open University Press). She is currently directing an ESRC funded project on the impact of formula funding on schools.

Margaret Maden is County Education Officer in Warwickshire where she has worked since 1987. Previously she worked in the LEA as Headteacher of

Islington Green Comprehensive School, as director of Islington Sixth Form Centre and as the Authority's Principal Adviser for Tertiary Planning. She has also been a regular contributor to the *Times Educational Supplement, Education*, and other media.

Rob McBride was a head of department in an ILEA secondary school before conducting research in a large, DES funded project. He has been employed at the University of East Anglia since October 1987, becoming a Senior Research Associate in CARE and then a member of faculty in the School of Education. In 1989 he edited *The In-Service Training of Teachers* (Falmer Press) and has contributed papers to a number of publications and conferences. Currently he is researching INSET, professional work and its management, and health education. He is also a practising evaluator.

Robert McGovern has taught secondary, junior and middle school pupils for the past fifteen years. He has a particular interest in curriculum development and the management of primary schools. He is currently a Senior Lecturer in Education at Derbyshire College of Higher Education.

David Shearn took a degree in mathematics and an MA in Operational Research. After nine years in the steel industry he took up his current post as a Lecturer in OR, and now teaches in the area of computer-based information systems and business statistics. He has conducted a number of studies in non-profit organisations and education. He is Chair of Governors of a large comprehensive school which has successfully taken on local management.

Mike Stewart is currently the Local Management Manager for the South Kent Area, with responsibility for the introduction of LM into the Area's 150 schools. He has been a secondary school teacher for fifteen years and moved into Educational Administration with the creation of his present post in 1989. He is undertaking research into the impact of LM and the changes it is bringing to educational management.

Gwen Wallace is a Principal Lecturer and Head of Social Sciences at Derbyshire College of Higher Education. Her major research interest lies in the relationship between organisational contexts and human behaviour and she has contributed papers to a number of books and journals. She has served for a number of years on the Executive Council of the British Educational Research Association. Prior to moving to Derbyshire in 1981, she worked on an SSRC funded project on middle schools at the University of Aston. She has thirteen years' experience of teaching in secondary schools.